Contents

Introduction

Italian Lakes ...5
Historical Highlights ...10

Places

Route 1: Lake Maggiore ...14
Route 2: Lake Maggiore – Varese – Como ...25
Route 3: Lake Lugano ...28
Route 4: Como ...35
Route 5: Lake Como ...39
Route 6: Bergamo ...49
Route 7: Lake Iseo ...51
Route 8: Lake Garda ...55
Route 9: Verona ...74

Culture

Art History ...79
Festivals ...82

Leisure

Food and Drink ...85
Active Holidays ...90

Practical Information

Getting There ...93
Getting Around ...94
Facts for the Visitor ...95
Accommodation ...99

Index ...104

Italian Lakes – A Region for all Tastes

The Northern Italian Lakes are one of the most fascinating regions of Italy, and also one of the most popular with tourists. Their waters ensure that winters stay pleasantly mild, and summers pleasantly cool. Their shores are lined with elegant villas surrounded by delightful parks and gardens. The region is also justly famed for its magnificent views and vistas, and a drive through this part of Italy is often a challenge to intrepid motorists as well as being an unforgettable visual treat.

The Northern Italian Lakes – Maggiore, Como, Lugano, Garda and the many smaller ones – are surrounded by the Swiss Ticino and the Italian regions of Lombardy and Piedmont, all of them areas steeped in history and with no end of superb cultural sights to visit, ranging from prehistoric remains and Roman ruins to finely-crafted Lombard Romanesque churches and magnificent Renaissance architecture. The lakes region, where Italy meets the Alps and northern Europe, has always been of enormous strategic importance historically, and the beautiful landscape is enhanced still further by dozens of castles and fortresses, including those built by Verona's most famous medieval family, the Scaligeri, along the shores of Lake Garda. Verona has almost as many as Rome itself, while Bergamo owes its architectural beauty and harmony to the many years of Venetian rule there. These cities and also many of the smaller towns contain first-class art galleries, with priceless paintings by artists such as Titian, Raphael, Tintoretto and Mantegna.

In the days before mass tourism, Lake Como in particular was a holiday retreat for British connoisseurs of good taste, including writers. Wordsworth lived there in 1790, Byron and Shelley were both regular visitors, and DH Lawrence made it his home from 1925 to 1927. Visitors today can not only bask in the extraordinary cultural landscape and scenery that the region possesses, but also enjoy many activities associated with a modern tourist infrastructure, such as windsurfing, waterskiing or golf. Hikers and climbers can take to the mountains, while those in search of relaxation can sunbathe on the shore or enjoy the spectacular views from the deck of a steamer. In addition to all this, the region is justly famed for its food and also its wines, many of which bear familiar names such as *Bardolino*, *Valpolicella* and *Soave*.

These are just a few of the reasons why the Italian Lakes have exerted such an irresistable attraction on tourists for so many years now. And last but not least of course, there are the Italians themselves – happy, spontaneous and friendly. Welcome to one of the most beautiful and exciting parts of Italy.

Opposite: Isola di Garda

Views wherever you look

Villa d'Este at Cernobbio

Grotte di Catullo on Lake Garda

Position and landscape

The lakes lie in Upper Italy between the Lombardy Plain and the high Alps. Each lake has its own individual character and shape: they are all long and thin (known as ribbon lakes), but Maggiore, the second largest lake (66km/41 miles long), has a kink in it like the hind leg of a horse, Lugano and Como resemble upside down 'Y's, while Garda, the largest lake (51km/33 miles long), has a bulbous bottom, like a retort. All these shapes are the result of complex local geology and the process of glaciation that took place during the Ice Age (*see below*). While the southern end of Lake Garda extends into the plain, Lake Como is surrounded by mountains. Even though it is only the third-largest lake in Upper Italy (50km/32 miles long), Como is actually the deepest inland lake in Europe (410m/1,350ft).

Val Cannobina

Though not as high as the central Alps, the mountains surrounding the lakes provide an impressive backdrop. The summit of Monte Legnone (2,609m/8,560ft) towers more than 2,400m (7,900ft) over the surface of Lake Como – at a horizontal distance of only 6km (4 miles) from the shore. It is the highest summit in the region described, but there are other impressive and beautiful massifs around Como, notably the limestone Grigna (2,409m/7,903ft). The Ticino Alps around Maggiore to the west, though not quite so high, still have some fine peaks, including the Gridone (2,188m/ 7,178ft) and Monte Zeda (2,156m/ 7,070ft). Away to the east, Lake Garda is separated from the Adige valley by the narrow ridge of Monte Baldo which rises almost 2,000m (6,500ft) above the lake.

Lake Maggiore is drained by the Ticino river, Lake Como by the Adda, Lake Garda by the Mincio. All of them are tributaries of the Po, which flows into the Adriatic.

Diving into Lake Garda

Geology

Some 350 million years ago, much of present day Upper Italy was covered by a tropical sea. As the marine life died it was deposited on the sea bed, where it consolidated in layers, until around 60 million years ago when massive movements of the earth's crust resulted in the creation of the Alps. Around 2 million years ago, during the Pleistocene period, the rivers that flowed into the Po from the Apennines and the Alps brought a great deal of alluvial silt with them; this was deposited on the Plain of Lombardy and is the reason why the whole area has remained so fertile to this day.

Prior to the last Ice Age, there were no lakes in the region, but simply large valleys. During this Ice Age the rivers became powerful glaciers, and massive basins were gouged out of the rock. The level of the bottom of these new basins was considerably lower than that of the exit to the valleys, so after the glaciers retreated and the valleys filled up with water, the resultant lakes were extremely deep, their bottoms lying well below sea level. Additional depth was created by the morraine debris the glaciers left behind as they retreated. The deepest part of Lake Garda, for instance, is 346m (1,135ft), with the moraine thickness of 149m (488ft) making up almost half of that. The glaciers left behind not only lakes but also highly complex drainage patterns, seen, for example in the two arms of Lake Como, one of which has no outflow at all, and in Lake Orta to the west of Lake Maggiore, which drains out to the north.

Isola di Garda

The mountains defining the lakes are not of uniform structure. To the north of Lake Garda, they are formed of a specialised form of limestone known as Dolomite. Between Garda and Como, the prevalent rock is granite, whose resistance to erosion explains the fact that no large lake has been formed in that area. Around Como and Maggiore, it's largely limestone again, though intrusions of crystalline rock (schists and gneiss) become more pronounced the further west you go.

Climate and when to go

The Mediterranean type climate of the Italian lakes is one of the main reasons tourists are so attracted to the area. Despite their proximity to the Alps and central European location, the lakes are so large that they actually distort the local climate, making winters warmer than is usual for this latitude and summers slightly cooler. However, because of the mountain environment the weather on Lakes Maggiore, Como and particularly Garda isn't all that predictable: in spring and autumn, be prepared for sudden cloudbursts (most likely to occur in May and September).

Como: Villa dell'Olmo and Tempio Voltano

Tremezzo: Villa Carlotta gardens

Formal gardens in Verona

Even in January, snowfalls are very rare at lake level, and by the beginning of April the sun is as warm as it is elsewhere in Europe in mid-May. In the summer a fresh breeze keeps the temperatures pleasant even when there isn't a cloud in the sky. The relatively steady winds blowing up and down the lakes make them a paradise for windsurfers and sailors.

The water is also a very pleasant 25°C (77°F) during July and August. Many like to visit the lakes in the springtime, when there is a profusion of blossom and the villas with their parks and gardens are utterly magnificent. Swimmers tend to favour early summer through to September as a good time for a holiday. Autumn is ideal for long hikes and serene contemplation of (relatively) tourist-free scenery, and the service is a lot better in the restaurants because the staff have more time. Winter is quiet, and many places close down for the season.

Summer grazing

Flora and fauna

In January, when everything north of the Alps is usually under a blanket of snow, rose, jasmine and laurels are already blooming in Northern Italy. In February, the mimosa and forsythia herald the spring with their intense yellow blossom, and in March the camellias, magnolias, oleander, gorse and peach-trees all burst into blossom. The whole scene is quite Mediterranean, and it's hard to believe that such splendour actually exists miles inland. The vegetation is as varied as the local fauna. Reptiles are common, especially lizards and the odd snake. A lot of animals are active at night, such as wild pigs, foxes and bats. All lakes have an abundance of fish, including trout, eel, carp and whitefish, though until urgent remedial action was recently taken by the authorities, stocks were under serious threat from water pollution.

Language

Un omm al gheva a düü fiö ('A man had two sons') could be the opening of any local fairytale, and anyone who's just done a course in Italian will be annoyed to discover that he doesn't understand a word. The strange language is Lombardian. Never fear, however: only a few small communities high in the mountains continue to communicate in it. The language of Dante – which marked the beginning of Italian literature – was Tuscan, and over the centuries Lombardian was gradually squeezed out by Tuscan Italian as the favoured dialect.

Friendly locals

Rural lifestyles

Economy

Lombardy is considered the 'powerhouse of Italy', and so it's no wonder that the towns along the edge of the Alps (Varese, Como, Lecco) are largely industrial. The most obviously industrial areas are in the Brianza and around Como; the latter, famous as the *città della seta* (city of silk), has diversified a lot over the past few decades and become as industrial as Varese. Ironworking has taken over from silk as the main industry around Lake Como.

As far as agriculture is concerned, the higher plains are suited to the cultivation of cereals, including maize (for polenta), green vegetables, fruit trees and mulberries (for silk cocoons). The hilly zone has fruit and chestnut trees, and the soil around the lakes is especially suitable for olive trees and limes. Vines grow to an altitude of 850m (2,400ft), and on the Alpine meadows there is excellent grazing for both cattle (half of which are milk producing) and sheep (bred for wool as well as meat).

Vineyards in Custoza

A vital part of economy is tourism. Lake Garda alone has 5 million foreign visitors a year. The sheer wealth of cultural sights combined with the astonishing variety of activities on offer acts as an irresistible magnet to tourists from all over the world; one reason why summer accommodation beside any of the lakes these days should be booked at least six months in advance.

However, not all the inhabitants of the region have gained from its prosperity. Whenever you travel a short distance inland from the roads around these lakes it becomes clear just how deserted many of the villages in the rural areas have become. The steep peaks and deep ravines, so picturesque for the traveller, are often part of a never-ending struggle for survival for the poor people living in regions like the Grigna. Young people have been leaving for the towns and big cities to set up a new life for themselves in safer and more comfortable surroundings. Only recently has there been a movement among young people *away* from the smog and hectic lifestyle and back to the peace of the countryside – and it is growing steadily more popular.

Historical Highlights

9,000BC Settlers arrive in the fertile Po Plain as the ice sheets withdraw.

7th century BC The Celts head southwards, and their settlements later develop into some of Northern Italy's finest cities, including Milan, Como and Bergamo. The Celts trade busily with the Etruscans, who cross the Apennines as far as Mantua.

4th century BC The Gauls cross the Alps, sacking Rome in 390BC.

3rd century BC The Romans move northwards to drive out the Gauls and bring the whole of northern Italy under their control.

191BC The region becomes the Roman province of Gallia Cisalpina. The capital is Mediolanum (Milan), vital as a strategic crossroads between territories to the east, west and south, as well as a springboard for future expansion to the north. The Romans lay the foundations of the industrial triangle between Milan, Genoa and Turin.

2nd century BC Bergamo and Como both become Roman colonies.

89BC Verona becomes a Roman colony.

59–49BC Under the governorship of Caesar, Verona, too, becomes a strategically important crossroads and develops into a major administrative and commercial centre.

AD286 Diocletian assigns Milan as residence and main administrative centre to his emperor-colleague, Maximian.

AD313 Under the Edict of Milan, Constantine the Great grants freedom of worship to Christians.

4th century AD The Upper Italian lake area becomes a transit region for French and English pilgrims on their way to Rome.

AD330 Constantine moves the capital of the Empire to Byzantium.

5th century Following the division of the Empire into two halves in 393, the western part becomes weakened and vulnerable to attacks by the warlike tribes of central Europe.

403 Verona is besieged by the Visigoths under Alaric.

452 The forces of Attila the Hun lay waste to Verona and the Po Plain.

476 End of the western Empire. The Germanic leader Odoacer conquers northern Italy.

568 The Lombards, a Teutonic tribe, invade northern Italy. Within a year they have conquered all the cities north of the River Po, and soon assume control of the lakes region, and call it Lombardy. In the latter part of the 7th century, the Lombards are converted to Christianity by Theodolinda, daughter of a Bavarian duke.

774 After the invasion of the papal territories by the Lombard kings, Charlemagne is summoned by the pope. He destroys the Lombard kingdom and creates a Frankish state in northern Italy.

9th–10th centuries Bishops of cities such as Bergamo and Como obtain a succession of sovereign privileges, exercising civil as well as ecclesiastical rule over entire districts.

962 Otto the Great retakes Italy, heralding the start of almost 200 years of attempted German domination in the area.

11th–16th centuries The period of the Italian city states. In northern Italy, Milan, Bergamo and Verona all begin to thrive from the burgeoning overland trade with the Orient. At first, power is in the hands of the merchants, but later belongs to just a few local families (*Signori*). In Verona and Garda it is the della Scalas (Scaligeri), in Milan the Visconti.

11th–12th centuries Having declared itself an autonomous commune, in the ensuing struggle for primacy among the cities of Lombardy,

Milan becomes involved in a series of long battles against its less prosperous neighbours.

1118–27 In the Ten Years' War, Milan virtually destroys Como.

1164 The Veronese League is formed to combat attempts by Emperor Frederick Barbarossa to bring the Lombard cities under his control. It forms the basis of the Lombard League, established in 1167.

1176 Frederick Barbarossa is defeated by the Lombard League at Legnano. By the Peace of Constance in 1183, he is forced to accept the independence of the city states as free communes.

1262 The rise of the Scaligeri family of Garda begins when Mastino I della Scala becomes mayor of Verona, the first Scaligeri to rise to a position of prominence in the Garda region.

1277 Mastino I della Scala is murdered, but the Venetians immediately replace him by his tyrannical brother, Alberto.

1278–1447 The Visconti in power in Milan.

1311–29 Cangrande I della Scala extends his sphere of influence, and soon his court is one of the most magnificent in all Italy.

1335 The Visconti take over Como.

1352 The hated Cangrande II della Scala assumes power, and is murdered seven years later by his brother Cansignorio.

1387 Scaligeri rule comes to an end when Verona is besieged by the Visconti.

1405–1521 Venice conquers Verona and Lake Garda.

1450 Francesco Sforza, son-in-law of the last Visconti, assumes power in Milan and Como.

1496–1500 The area of modern-day Ticino is annexed to Switzerland.

1500–25 Milan is a bone of contention between France, Germany and Venice. Emperor Charles V installs another Sforza as duke.

1535 After the death of the last Sforza duke, Milan falls to Spain.

1796 Napoleon conquers Lombardy and the Veneto. One year later the Cisalpine Republic is formed at the Treaty of Campoformio.

1814–15 Napoleon is defeated. At the Congress of Vienna, Lombardy and the Veneto are ceded to Austria.

Early 19th century The Italians of the north under Austrian rule and the 'free' Italians of the kingdom of Piedmont begin to campaign for an independent Italy. In 1842, a newspaper called *Il Risorgimento* (*The Awakening*) is published, after which the independence movement takes its name. It is led by Giuseppe Garibaldi.

1848–66 The Risorgimento fights against Austrian rule.

1859 After losing several of their early battles, the freedom fighters gain a decisive victory at the bloody Battle of Solferino, south of Lake Garda.

1861 Vienna is finally forced to surrender Lombardy and the Veneto to the newly-founded Kingdom of Italy.

1919 Under the terms of the Treaty of Saint-Germain, Austria loses the northern shore of lake Garda, the Trentino and also the southern Tyrol. Reunified Italy now extends as far as the Brenner Pass. Benito Mussolini establishes the first fascist brigades in Milan. The fascists come to power three years later.

1943–45 After the collapse of the northern front, Mussolini retires to Lake Garda and founds the short-lived 'Republic of Salò'. On 28 April 1945 the Duce and his mistress Clara Petacci are caught by partisans while trying to flee to Switzerland, and are summarily executed.

1946 Italy becomes a republic.

1993 Catastrophic floods at Lake Maggiore.

Taking the high road

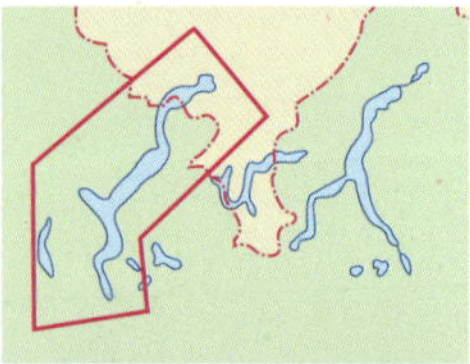

Smile from Val Cannobina

Preceding pages: Lake Orta

Route 1

★★ Lake Maggiore

Lake Maggiore, the *Lacus Verbanus* of Ancient Rome, much praised as a natural wonder and a popular holiday destination for generations, is for many the epitome of the South, of *Bella Italia*. Like all the lakes south of the Alps, Lake Maggiore owes its existence to Ice Age glaciers which hollowed out its base to a depth of 372m (1,220ft) – or a full 179m (587ft) below sea-level. With a surface area of 216sq m (2,324sq ft), Lake Maggiore is the second-largest of the Northern Italian Lakes after Lake Garda; it is 66km (41 miles) long, but has an average width of between 4km (2 miles) and 11km (6 miles). The lake's most important river is the Ticino, which has its source in the Alps of Central Switzerland and flows into Lake Maggiore near Locarno. The Ticino river also drains the lake, flowing into the Po not far from Pavia.

Lake Maggiore is shared by Italy and Switzerland: the upper fifth of it is Swiss and forms part of the canton of Ticino; the western shore is part of the Italian region of Piedmont (province of Novara); and the eastern shore belongs to Lombardy (province of Varese). The northern part of the lake, surrounded by high mountains such as the Gridone (2,188m/7,180ft), opens up more and more towards the south, unveiling its special attractions as it does so. The mountains form a grand backdrop, and the southern sun bathes the landscape in brilliant light.

But Lake Maggiore isn't just sunshine, water and mountains: its villas and parks, now magnificent museums, are reminders of the old days when people travelled from Milan to the lake by coach, and travel was the privilege of a small section of society. Today all that pomp and

ROUTE 1
0
5 km
N
SWITZERLAND
ITALY
Piedmont
Lombardy
Centovalli
Val Vigezzo
Val Cannobina
Valtravaglia
Valcuvia
Valganna
Val Verzasca
Val Veddasca
VERGANTE
Lago Maggiore
Lago di Lugano
Lago di Varese
Lago di Monate
Lago di Comabbio
Lago di Vogorno
Lago Delio
Locarno
Ascona
Muralto
Minusio
Brione
Brè
Cimetta
1671
Ronco
Brissago
Isole di Brissago
S. Nazzaro
Vira
Magadino
Gerra
Riazzogna
M. Gambarogno
1734
C. di Neggia
1395
S. Abbondio
Caviano
Zenna
Indemini
M. Tamaro
1962
M. Gridone
(M. Limidario)
2188
Malesco
Piano di Sale
934
Finero
1846
Testa del Mater
Gurro
Falmenta
M. Giove
1298
Sant'Agata
Orrido di Sant'Anna
Cannobio
Carmine
Maccagno
M. Bogna
1157
Curiglia
Agra
M. Lema
1620
Dumenza
Castelli d. C.
Trarego
Cannero Riviera
Luino
Germignaga
Oggebbio
Cima della Laurasca
2195
M. Zeda
2156
Riserva Naturale Val Grande
Cicogna
Miazzina
Premeno
Ghiffa
Trobaso
Porto Valtravaglia
Brezzo d. Bedero
Caldè
Castelveccana
Ponte Tresa
Tresa
M. Rosso
693
Verbania
Intra
Pallanza
Baveno
Isole Borromee
Laveno
1062
S.so del Ferro
M. Nudo
1235
Ghirla
Cerro
Reno
Mombello
Stresa
Alpino
Gignese
Parco d. Campo d. Fiori
M. Campo d. Fiori
1226
Arcisate
Besozzo
Gavirate
Belgirate
Lesa
Massino Visconti
Ispra
Brebbia
Travedona
Varese
Malnate
Ranco
412
S. Quirico
Cadrezzate
Meina
Angera
Arona
Sesto Calende
Vergiate
Castelletto
Golasecca
Ticino
Toce
Maggia
Giona
Olona
Domodossola
M. Mottarone
St. Gotthard Pass
S. Bernardino Pass
Lugano
Como
Novara
Milano
1a
1b
1c

grandeur is history; increasing traffic and industry make smog-free days something of a rarity.

With its towns of Locarno, Ascona, Verbania and Stresa, the Piedmont shore is more wealthy than the less developed eastern shore. The latter, on the other hand, has more unspoilt natural scenery. The prosperity of the western shore means no less than a third of the working population on the eastern shore of Lake Maggiore work in Switzerland, and commute between the two countries daily.

Lakeshore at Locarno

1a – The Western Shore

Locarno – Ascona – Brissago – Cannobio – Verbania (57km/35 miles) *See map, p15*

★★ **Locarno** (pop. 17,000) vies with Lugano for the title of finest town in the Ticino. The magnificent landscape at the upper end of Lake Maggiore and the mild, fog-free climate attracted Northern European tourists here from the end of the 19th century onwards. The town prospered after World War II, and now includes the suburbs of Muralto, Minusio, Orselina and Brione. Today the shore of Lake Maggiore is built up from the Maggia to the Verzasca, but Locarno still retains much of its charm – a special combination of Swiss-Alpine and Southern-Italian.

The region round Locarno was probably inhabited during prehistoric times, but was certainly settled during the Roman era. The first written mention of the town dates from AD789. Over the centuries, Locarno profited from its strategic location at the northern end of Lake Maggiore, on the trading route leading across the great Alpine passes. It received its charter from the emperor Barbarossa in 1189, and passed into the hands of the Viscontis of Milan in 1342. In 1513 it was conquered by the Swiss Confederation, and after the fall of the Ancien Regime (1798) it became a part of the Swiss canton of Lugano. From 1803 to 1878 it then shared the status as Ticino's capital alternately with Lugano and Bellinzona. The town became famous from the Treaty of Locarno, signed in 1925, which allowed Germany back into the League of Nations after World War I.

Aspects of the Piazza Grande

At the centre of Locarno is the **Piazza Grande**, where the traditional weekly market is held every second Tuesday; the square dates from the 19th century. The 14th-century Torre del Comune forms part of the line of houses on the side facing the mountains; to the east is the municipal park with the theatre. Down the Via Franchino Rusca is the ★ **Castello**, still one of the most important castles in the Ticino despite being largely destroyed by the Confederation in 1532. It was founded in medieval times, and today houses the **Museo Civico** (April to October Tuesday to Sunday 10am–noon, 2–5pm) with its extensive collections of local archaeological finds and Romanesque sculpture. The historic town centre is a great place for a stroll: one of the finest townhouses is the **Casa Rusca**, which contains the Pinacoteca Comunale (9am–noon and 2–5pm) with the important Dada collection by Hans Arp.

Of the churches in the old town, **Santa Maria in Selva** is well known for its Late Gothic ★ choir frescoes, showing *Scenes from the Life of Christ*, but the most famous sacred structure on the northern shore of Lake Maggiore is definitely the church of ★★ **San Vittore** in Muralto, not far from the railway station. This three-aisled Romanesque pillared basilica dates from between 1090 and 1110, and the Romanesque ★★ crypt with its fascinating capitals is definitely worth a visit.

Monk at Madonna del Sasso

Above Locarno stands the famous pilgrimage church of **Madonna del Sasso**, the site of which doubles as a superb observation point for the city, mountains and lake. It can be reached by road or by tram, or, for the more energetic, by the old Way of the Cross. The present pilgrimage church of Santa Maria Assunta dates from the 16th and 17th centuries, and the main attraction of the interior is Bramantino's *Flight from Egypt* (1520).

Hidden Ascona

The mighty delta of the Maggia separates Locarno from the no less beautiful town of ★ **Ascona** (pop. 4,800). Still only a small fishing village before the turn of the century, Ascona first became a paradise for theosophical 'seekers after truth' before becoming the cosmopolitan resort it is today. Picturesquely situated in a bay, the town has an unmistakeable flair of its own, despite the annual tourist invasion. The parish church of **SS Pietro e Paolo**, a 16th-century three-aisled pillared basilica, contains three magnificent ★ altar paintings by the local painter Giovanni Serodine (1594–1630), who lived next door in Ascona's finest baroque building, the ★ **Casa Borrani** (1620). At the edge of the old town centre is the **Collegio Paio**, founded in 1584, with a fine Renaissance courtyards and a magnificent ★ cloister. The church of **Santa Maria della Misericordia** contains several valuable ★ frescoes dating from the 15th and 16th centuries.

Collegio Paio: the cloister

High above Ascona is **Monte Verità** (321m/1,050ft), with a view across the lake and the Maggia delta. The **Casa Anatta** (April to October Tuesday to Sunday 2.30–6pm, July to August 3–7pm), headquarters of the 'Vegetarian Cooperative of Ascona' from 1900 to 1920, contains much information on all the reformists and communards who came here to 'get away from it all' earlier this century.

Casa Anatta exhibits

The nearby town of **Brissago** has a very southern atmosphere, with all its palazzi and Mediterranean vegetation. Archaeological finds in the vicinity point to early settlement by the Celts, who were followed by the Romans. During the Middle Ages, Brissago was a miniature republic and enjoyed several privileges such as tax exemption and its own legal system – rights which had to be fiercely defended during the 16th and 17th centuries, after it had joined the Confederation. Today, tourism is Brissago's main source of income, and the historic centre is consequently losing much of its former charm. Sights worth seeing include the **Casa Branca** (1680–1720) with its magnificent facade; the church of ★ **Madonna del Ponte** (1520–45) just to the south of the town, a fine example of Lombardian architecture; and the famous **cigar factory** (Fabbrica Tabacchi) founded in 1847, also south of the town (guided tours from May to September).

Madonna del Ponte

The region around Brissago is ideal for hiking, with some fine views of the lake and the mighty massif of the Gridone (2,188m/7,180ft) in the distance. Don't miss the ★ **Brissago Islands**, either. They were probably inhabited as far back as Roman times, and a ruined church on the Isolino (the smaller island) dates from the 12th century. The Isola Grande has a magnificent ★ **botanical garden** (guided tours April to September), with some unique tropical and subtropical vegetation. The villa, built in Italian Renaissance style in 1927, today houses an art museum (daily 9.30am–5.30pm).

Ferry to Isola Grande

Across the border in Italy, **Cannobio** is a delightful place, with a historic centre, picturesque arcades next to the lake and the pilgrimage church of **Santa Pietà** adjacent to the quayside. Built according to the plans of Pellegrino Tibaldi in 1571, it contains a miracle-working image of the *Mourning of Christ*. The 13th-century **Palazzo delle Ragione**, the old town hall, houses a small local museum.

Market day in Cannobio

Barely 2km (1½ miles) from the town centre, the Cannnobino stream crashes through the wild ★ **Orrido Sant'Anna** gorge. Slicing between the Gridone and Monte Zeda, the ★★ **Val Cannobina** itself is well worth a detour, with tiny settlements and the occasional church clinging to the mountainsides. Up this valley, a curiosity of a very special kind is the village of **Gurro**, whose inhabitants can be proud of their Scottish ancestry. After the Battle of Pavia in 1525, a company of Scottish mercenaries fighting on the side of the French decided to flee to this remote valley, where they settled down to a life of mountain farming and married the local girls. Even today, the local dialect contains elements of the gaelic tongue, and kilts are worn at festivals. Further evidence of the Scottish influence is to be found in the **museum** at Gurro (daily except Thursday 9am–5pm), as well as in the names of such establishments as the **Scotch Bar** and **Ristorante Scozia**.

Val Cannobina

Continuing down the western shore, just before the popular resort of Cannero Riviera, two rocky islands, the **Castelli di Cannero**, jut out of the water. They were once the stronghold of the notorious Mazzarditi brothers, who took over the existing castles on the islands in the early 15th century and terrorised lake travellers and lakeside dwellers with their piracy. The castles were razed to the ground in 1414 by Filippo Visconti; only the ruins remain.

From **Cannero Riviera** it is possible to take the mountain road to Verbania via Trarego, the Passo della Piazza and Premeno, but this route is only recommended for experienced mountain drivers. The route along the shore, which continues through **Oggebbio** and **Ghiffa**, has its own wonderful panoramas, including, over on the eastern shore, the cliffs of **Rocca di Caldè** (*see page 24*).

1b – The Piedmont Shore

Verbania – Baveno – Stresa – Lake Orta – Arona – Sesto Calende (91km/57 miles) *See map, p20*

The Piedmont shore of Lake Maggiore is definitely the most cultural and traditional one, as evidenced by its many villas. It is proud to have been visited by many well-known historical figures, including Queen Victoria.

Pallanza: blooms in Villa Taranto

The town of ★ **Verbania** (pop. 31,000) derives its name from the original Roman name for the lake: *Lacus Verbanus*. The two main sections of the town are Intra and ★ **Pallanza**; the former is rather industrial, while the latter is cosmopolitan, and one of the best known resorts on the lake. Pallanza, delightfully situated at the foot of the Monte Rosso, is separated from Intra by the Punta della

Castagnola and also by the large park surrounding the ★★ **Villa Taranto** (daily April to October 8.30am–7.30pm). This park is one enormous botanical garden, containing one of the richest collections of subtropical flora in Italy. Rhododendron, beech, tulips, magnolia, dahlias, azaleas all grow here in profusion among the leaping fountains. The park originally belonged to a Scottish nobleman, Neil McEacharn, who bequeathed it to the Italian state on his death in 1964.

The most important structure in Pallanza itself lies north of the Borgo, or old town, on the Viale G A Azari: the church of ★ **Madonna di Campagna**. Originally built 'in the fields', the church's original beauty has been somewhat marred today by industrial buildings nearby. Originally Romanesque, the church underwent Renaissance alteration during the early 16th century. The octagonal cupola with its pillared gallery is an unusual feature, and the Romanesque campanile is also striking. Highlights inside the building include choir stalls dating from 1582 and also several 16th-century frescoes.

The landscape around Verbania is a good example of just how varied the Italian lake region is. Just a few miles from the crowded lake promenade, the magnificent valleys and mountains are breathtakingly peaceful. The summit of the Monte Rosso (693m/2,273ft) with its view across the Gulf of Borromeo can very nearly be reached by car along a narrow road from the Viale G A Azari. ★ **Monte Zeda** (2,156m/7,070ft) near Miazzina provides an even more impressive panorama.

Lake Maggiore's so-called 'riviera' extends from Verbania around the Bay of Borromeo as far as Stresa. This fertile strip of land with its profusion of subtropical vegetation is best visited in early spring or late autumn when there are less tourists around; the views in clear weather can extend as far as the Swiss Alps at these times of year.

The pinkish granite quarried near the town of ★ **Baveno** (pop. 4,500) was used in the construction of St Paul's Basilica in Rome and the Galleria Vittorio Emanuele II in Milan. Baveno's Romanesque parish church and octagonal Renaissance baptistery are worth a visit, and the town is also famous as a health spa: Queen Victoria, Crown Prince Frederick, the later German emperors and Richard Wagner all stayed here at different times.

Borromean Islands from Baveno

The promenade in Baveno provides unique views of the famous ★★ **Borromean Islands.** These four islands between Baveno, Stresa and Pallanza still exert a magic attraction. The **Isola Bella** in particular has been praised by scores of writers and poets, including Dumas and Stendhal. The magic of the Isola Bella is definitely man-made, however: the idea of shaping the rocky island into a ship could have come straight from the Walt Disney workshop. It was Antonio Crivelli from Ponte Tresa, however, who turned the island into a complete work of art on the order of Carlo Borromeo III and his wife Isabella d'Abba. The **Palazzo Borromeo** (daily April to October 9am–noon and 1.30–5.30pm), partly designed by Carlo Fontana, contains several majestic halls and also the famous grottoes. The terraced ★ **baroque park** is the real highlight, however, with its delightful mix of subtropical flora and white peacocks; the dream-like beauty of the whole place is marred only by all the kitsch and souvenirs on sale. The **Isola dei Pescatori**, despite some fine flora, is rather the worse for wear, with its narrow streets and very expensive seafood restaurants. The **Isola Madre** – the largest of the four islands – has some fine vegetation and also a stylish 16th-century Palazzo Borromeo containing an interesting ceramics collection (daily April to October 9am–noon and 1.30–5.30pm). The fourth island, the **Isola San Giovanni**, is privately owned.

Isola Bella: the baroque park

★ **Stresa** (pop. 5,000), one of the most elegant resorts in Italy during the 19th century, is rather past its prime today. Nevertheless, many of the grand hotels still retain some of their former splendour from the days when crowned heads, famous artists and wealthy aristocrats were regular visitors; the American author Ernest Hemingway wrote his novel *Another Country* here. The view across the lake from the *Lungolago* (promenade) is a must: it takes in the Borromean Islands and also the opposite shore of Lake Maggiore as far as Monte Tamaro.

There are several good excursion possibilities around Stresa. Just outside the town on the road to Arona is the ★ **Villa Pallavicino** (April to October 9am–6pm) with its enormous park and zoo. For the energetic, the mountainous countryside between Lake Maggiore and Lake Orta has many numbered hiking routes – and if the weather gets wet, why not visit the ★ **Umbrella Museum** in Gignese (April to September Tuesday to Sunday 10am–noon and 3–6pm). The summit of the ★ **Monte Mottarone** (1,491m/4,891ft) above Stresa is a famous observation point, and can be reached by a toll road with several hairpins.

Villa Pallavicino

Much overshadowed by Lake Maggiore is the far smaller ★ **Lake Orta** in Piedmont. The Lago d'Orta was known to the Romans as *Lacus Cusius*, and is 13km (8 miles) long,

Basilica di San Giulio, details

Statue at Sacro Monte

Sesto Calende: Parco della Valle del Ticino

an average of 1.5km (1 mile) wide and measures 143m (470ft) at its deepest point. The steep alpine ranges of Valstrona and Val d'Ossola form a spectacular contrast to the rolling green hills below.

Romantically situated on the lake is ★ **Orta San Giulio** (294m/964ft; pop. 1,200). The baroque buildings around the central piazza are charming, but the real highlight is the small ★ **Isola di San Giulio** out in the lake, just 3 hectares (7 acres) in size, and dominated by the former episcopal palace and the ★ **Basilica di San Giulio**. Originally founded in around 390, today's structure is predominantly Romanesque. Don't miss the 12th-century black marble ★★ pulpit, still in excellent condition. Another sacred site in this region is the Franciscan monastery on the ★ **Sacro Monte** of Orta. There is a magnificent view from up here across the western bank of Lake Orta, and the outline of the 18th-century pilgrimage church of Madonna del Sasso can be made out in the distance.

From the southern shore of the lake it's not far to **Arona** (pop. 16,000), with its colossal ★ **statue** (20m/62ft high) of its most famous son, San Carlo Borromeo, looking out across Lake Maggiore. Cardinal Borromeo (1538–84), an ardent advocate of Catholicism, was canonised in 1610; this statue of him dates from 1697, and if you go up the spiral stairway and ladder inside you can look out of his eyes across the lake as far as the Varesotto.

At the southern end of Lake Maggiore is the industrial town of **Sesto Calende** (pop. 10,000), known to the Romans as *Sextum Calendarum*, and usually driven through very rapidly by most people today. The region was populated very early on, however, and fascinating archaeological finds dating from the 9th century BC and earlier can be examined in the **Museo Civico** (Tuesday to Saturday 8.30am–noon and 3–5pm, Sunday 10am–noon and 3–7pm). Sesto Calende isn't all industrial either – try visiting the ★ **Parco della Valle del Ticino**, a green oasis where the region's original natural scenery is still intact. The Ticino river leaves Lake Maggiore here, and innumerable species of bird (especially herons and swallows) nest along its banks.

1c – The Lombardian Shore

Sesto Calende – Angera – Laveno – Luino – Maccagno – Val Veddasca (80km/50miles) *See map, p15*

The eastern, Lombardian shore of Lake Maggiore is far removed from such noble resorts as Ascona or Stresa, and gardens and parks here are conspicuous by their absence. The eastern shore may be less spectacular, but it's far

Santa Caterina del Sasso

less spoilt and more rugged. The towns and small villages have so far successfully managed to escape the clutches of tourism, and are still largely owned by the local population. The hinterland is flat as far as Laveno, with several small communities dotted around, and further north the shore of the lake gets much steeper, becoming alpine in character but without losing that special Mediterranean character that makes Lake Maggiore so unique.

Angera (pop. 5,500), just 8km (5 miles) from Sesto Calende (*see page 22*), is a busy town situated in a pretty bay opposite Arona. The main highlight here is easily spotted: the ★ **Rocca di Angera** (April to October 9.30am–12.30pm and 2–6pm, July and August 9.30am–12.30pm and 3–7pm), a proud fortress up on a hill behind the town, with a commanding view across the countryside and the lake. The site is steeped in history: not far from the fortress is the cave known as the Antro di Mitra, where traces of the Mithraic cult (1st and 2nd centuries AD) were discovered. The castle dates back to the Torriani and the Visconti (14th century), and there are some fine ★ frescoes (1314) in the Gothic Sala della Giustizia depicting a Visconti victory. Don't forget to climb the tower – the view across to the Sacro Monte near Varese (*see page 15*) and the small island of Partegora is impressive.

Signposts along the eastern shore, not far from the tiny village of **Reno**, point the way to a place of pilgrimage: ★ **Santa Caterina del Sasso**. A 12th-century chapel on the site became a small Dominican monastery, which was miraculously spared destruction in the 17th century when a landslide stopped within feet of the church. The site immediately became a place of pilgrimage, but its guardian angels deserted it 270 years later in 1910 when another landslide smashed through the church roof. The church and the small monastery are at their most impressive when viewed from the lake.

Santa Caterina del Sasso: ceiling detail

From **Laveno** (pop. 9,000) there's a good view across the Gulf of Borromeo to the peaks of the Valais Alps. The town itself is industrial, but the local ceramic trade has a long history. In Cerro (3km/2 miles out of Laveno) the Civica Raccolta di Terraglia museum documents the development of this craft, introduced to the region in 1856.

Beyond Laveno is the 'Alpine' part of the eastern shore: the terrain gets steeper, and the narrow road starts going through several tunnels. Soon Castelveccana comes into view, along with the famous steep rock known as the **Rocca di Caldè** (373m/1,220ft). A castle once stood on top of the rock; it was razed by Confederation troops in 1513. Just before **Porto Valtravaglia** (pop. 2,500), which lies right beside the lake, there's an interesting alternative route (good views) via the villages of Nasca, Musadino and Muceno to **Brezzo di Bedero**. Brezza's 12th-century church of San Vittore still retains several of its Romanesque features.

Luino

Luino lies at the point where the valleys of the Tresa and the Travaglia meet Lake Maggiore, and is the industrial centre of the Lombardian shore. Luino's main attraction is its market, held every Wednesday. The area between the Piazza Garibaldi and the lake promenade is filled with all manner of fascinating wares for sale. Luino is thought to have been the birthplace of the Renaissance artist Bernadino Luini (1480–1532), but those expecting to see any works by the great painter here in Luino will be disappointed. The church of **San Pietro** in Campagna does have an *Adoration of the Magi* attributed to him, however. The Museo Civico in the Viale Dante contains several prehistoric finds from the region.

Hiking enthusiasts will enjoy the region around Luino, especially the ★ **Monte Lema** (1,620m/5,310ft) on the border with Ticino. There are marked routes from Dumenza and Curiglia to the summit. Motorists who don't mind hairpin bends can also travel as far as the Rifugio Campiglio (1,184m/3,884ft), from which the summit is only another 1½-hr hike. The view of Lakes Lugano and Maggiore from up here in good weather is superb.

Val Veddasca vernacular

At the confluence of the Veddasca Valley lies the resort of **Maccagno**, separated into upper and lower sections by the Giona stream. Apart from the lake, there are numerous excursion possibilities, including the scenic ★ **Val Veddasca**. The winding valley road leads to the almost deserted village of ★ **Indemni** just over the Swiss border, whose picturesque alleys and stone-roofed houses belie the fact that depopulation is a real problem in this part of the world. There are superb views as the road snakes its way down to **Vira** back on the lake.

Route 2

Lake-Hopping

Laveno – Varese – Como (48km/29 miles)

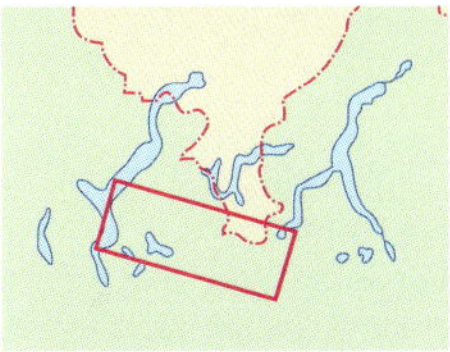

This connecting route between Lakes Maggiore and Como has several hidden attractions: the delightful Lake Varese, for instance, surrounded by attractive rolling hills; the provincial capital of Varese with its magnificent Sacro Monte; several fine mountain views; and Arcumeggia, a village that has become a very original art gallery. Plan a day for this trip.

Arcumeggia fresco

The first interesting detour on the route comes a few miles beyond Laveno: the little village of ★ **Arcumeggia**, where contemporary Italian artists have been busy reviving the ancient art of fresco painting. There are around 170 different frescoes on the houses here, and the place is well worth a visit. This region, known as the Valcuvia, has several other attractions: the 16th-century **Villa Bozzolo** in Casalzuigno with its magnificent park, the Romanesque campanile of **San Lorenzo** in the village of Cuveglio, and a ruined Sforza fortress above Orino on the northern slopes of the Monte Campo dei Fiori.

Going out in Gavirate

Travel on now via Gemonio (Romanesque church with frescoes) to **Gavirate** (pop. 8,000), picturesquely situated on the northern shore of **Lake Varese**. This 8-km (5-mile) long lake measures 4km (2 miles) at its widest point, and is extremely shallow (max depth 26m/85ft); its banks are thus rather marshy and this has spared it much new building construction. Wine is grown on the hills at the foot of **Monte Campo dei Fiori** (1,226m/4,020ft) and also

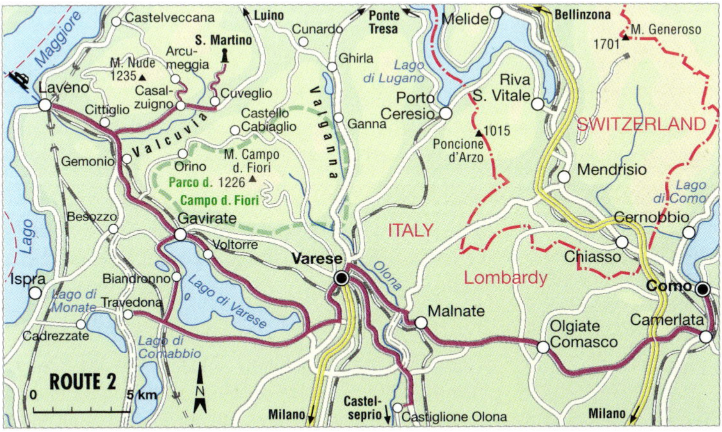

in the region south of the lake. To the southwest of lake Varese are two smaller lakes: Lake Comabbio and Lake Monate. A third one, Lake Biandronno, is almost completely dry now. Several remains of prehistoric lake dwellings have been discovered in this region, and finds can be seen in the **Museo Preistorico** (June to September Thursday to Sunday 3–6pm) on the tiny island of **Virgina** in Lake Varese, not far from Biandronno.

Fishing on Virgina

There are several fine cultural sights in the Lake Varese region, especially in **Voltorre** (2km/1½ miles from Gavirate), where the parish church of **San Michele** has a superb 12th-century Romanesque ★ cloister, and also in **Travedona** (7km/4 miles southwest of Gavirate on Lake Monate), with its church of **Santa Maria della Neve**.

The provincial capital of **Varese** (pop. 95,000) was still quite insignificant during the Middle Ages, but has now developed into a typically Northern Italian metropolis with a lot of industry but also a lot of old villas and parks. Varese lies in the region known as the Varesotto, which extends from Lake Lugano up to the edge of Greater Milan, and includes the famous Sacro Monte, Castiglione Olona and Castelseprio.

Unlike Como, the originally Gallo-Roman settlement of Varese hardly played any role in Lombard history; it only became a town in 1816. One of the most noticeable features of the town is the baroque campanile (77m/252ft) of the basilica of **San Vittore**, built between 1580 and 1615; the original Renaissance structure was given a neoclassical facade in 1788. The building contains frescoes by leading Lombard masters, and the neighbouring ★ **baptistery** has several fresco fragments dating from the 13th and 14th centuries.

Varese: Palazzo Estense

The old part of Varese is centred around San Vittore, but there's a sharp contrast just a short distance away in the Piazza Monte Grappa, where buildings dating from 1927 to 1935 all bear the unmistakeable stamp of Italian Fascist architecture. Northwest of the square, up the Via Sacco, is the 18th-century Austrian style **Palazzo Estense** (1776–83), reminiscent of Schoenbrunn in Vienna. Its owner, Francesco III d'Este, was the imperial governor of Austrian Lombardy and also Duke of Modena. Across the grounds in the **Villa Mirabello**, the Municipal Museum (Tuesday to Saturday 9.30am–noon and 2–5pm, Sunday 9am–12.30pm) contains an interesting prehistoric collection and also an art gallery.

One very good excursion from Varese is to the ★ **Sacro Monte** (880m/2,880ft) or 'Holy Mountain', a famous place of pilgrimage. A pilgrimage church was built on the mountain in the 10th century, and it was later used to house a statue of the Virgin, known as the Black Madonna because it is carved from dark wood. In the 16th century, plans were drawn up for a ★ **Via Crucis** (Way of the Cross), lined with chapels. Thanks to the skills of the architect Giuseppe Bernascone, who built the round domed structures at the beginning of the 17th century, the ascent along the 2-km (1½-mile) long cobbled route leading from the Prima Cappella to the church of Santa Maria del Monte is unforgettable. Art and landscape are harmoniously combined, and the chapels are decorated with many frescoes and several larger-than-life terracotta figures. The church of **Santa Maria del Monte** itself, in which the Black Madonna still stands, is a mixture of styles from Romanesque to baroque; its massive campanile is particularly striking, and the early 11th-century crypt contains some fine Gothic frescoes.

While in Varese, don't miss an excursion 11km (6 miles) southwards to ★★ **Castiglione Olona** (churches and museum Tuesday to Friday 10am–noon and 3–6pm, weekend 10am–12.30pm and 2.30–6pm), which today is a small and rather insignificant industrial town. During the Renaissance, however, it was turned into a kind of 'mini-Florence' in the middle of Lombardy by Cardinal Branda Castiglione (1350–1443). The numerous palazzi, including that of the cardinal himself, have lost much of their former glory, but the sacred buildings are magnificent. The ★ **Chiesa di Villa** (1422–43) is a centralised structure reminiscent of Brunelleschi's work in Florence, and the ★ **Collegiata**, reached by an idyllic walk, contains marvellous frescoes by the Florentine artist Masolino da Panicale (1435), who also painted the *Scenes from the Life of John the Baptist* in the ★ baptistery.

Not far away, at ★ **Castelseprio**, the large excavation site to the east of the village was probably a settlement founded by the Celtic Insubrians, then the capital of a Lombard province, and then a powerful medieval commune before its destruction by the Visconti in 1287. Several ruined walls have been exposed to view. The small church of Santa Maria Foris Portas nearby probably dates from the 7th century originally, and contains a magnificent ★ fresco cycle which, though incomplete, was painted somewhere between the 7th and 9th centuries.

To reach Lake Como from Varese, take the SS 342 via Malnate and Olgiate-Comasco. The most common type of building along this route is unfortunately the *supermercado*, but there's an interesting coach, steam train and bicycle museum in the Villa Rachele-Ogliari in **Malnate**, to add a welcome touch of nostalgia.

Sacro Monte: Way of the Cross and Santa Maria del Monte

Castiglione Olona

The lake from a Swiss perspective

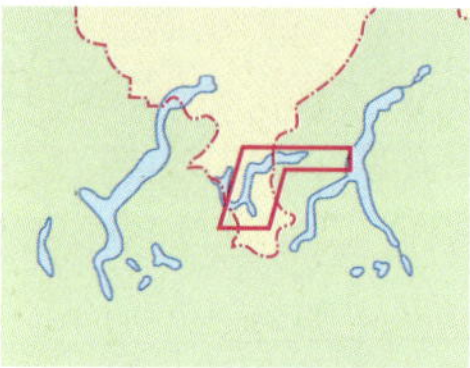

Route 3

★★ Lake Lugano

Lake Lugano is 271m (889ft) above sea-level, and measures 48.9sq km (19sq miles); three quarters of the lake lie in Ticino. With its strange shape and steep, rocky shores, Lake Lugano is rather reminiscent of Lake Lucerne minus the Alpine backdrop. The best view of the lake, which has an average width of less than 2km (1½ miles) can be had from the hills around Lugano, but for a proper experience of the *Ceresio*, as the locals refer to their lake, take a boat trip past the rocky mountain slopes. Unlike Lakes Como or Maggiore, the large amount of weed in Lake Lugano means that its dark-green water never appears transparent, even on sunny days.

Route 3a: Lugano to Como

Lugano – Melide – Morcote – Bissone– Capolago – Riva San Vitale – Mendrisio (32km/20 miles)

Lugano waterfront

★★ **Lugano** (pop. 29,000), the largest city in Ticino, is magnificently situated in its semicircular bay between the peaks of **Monte Brè** (925m/3,034ft) in the east and **Monte Salvatore** (912m/2,992ft) in the south. The wonderful mixture of stunning mountain scenery and mild, sunny climate has made the region around Lugano one of the most popular tourist areas in Switzerland, though the sheer speed of construction work during the past decades has also resulted in quite a number of negative developments.

Archaeological finds date the earliest settlement of the region back to pre-Roman times. The city received its first written mention (as *Luano*) in the year 818. During the Middle Ages Lugano was often involved in the struggles between Milan and Como. From 1803 to 1978 it alternated as the capital of Ticino with Bellinzona and Locarno.

The best place to start any tour of the city is the **Piazza della Riforma** with its elegant 19th-century buildings. The cafés here are popular meeting-places for young and old alike. The **Municipio**, or Town Hall, on the south side of the piazza dates from 1844, and the famous lake promenades lead southwards and eastwards towards Paradiso and the municipal park. Inland is the largely traffic-free city centre, where several old buildings still survive. The Via Pessina has picturesque arcades and typical cobblestones, and the Via Nassa, which joins it to the south, has now become the city's main shopping street. It comes out in the Piazza B Luini, named after the Renaissance painter several of whose works can be admired here in the church of ★★ **Santa Maria degli Angioli**. Built in 1515, the church belonged to a Franciscan monastery that was dissolved in 1848. The interior is dominated by Luini's enormous *Crucifixion*, which he completed in 1529 while under the influence of Leonardo da Vinci. Three other frescoes – the *Last Supper* on the south wall, and the *Mourning of Christ* and *Mary with Jesus and St John* – were originally painted by Luini for the monastery.

High above the old town is the ★ **Cathedral of San Lorenzo**. First mentioned as a parish church in 818, it dates back to an old Roman pillared basilica that was vaulted and extended in the 13th century before receiving its side

Encounters on the piazza

Santa Maria degli Angioli

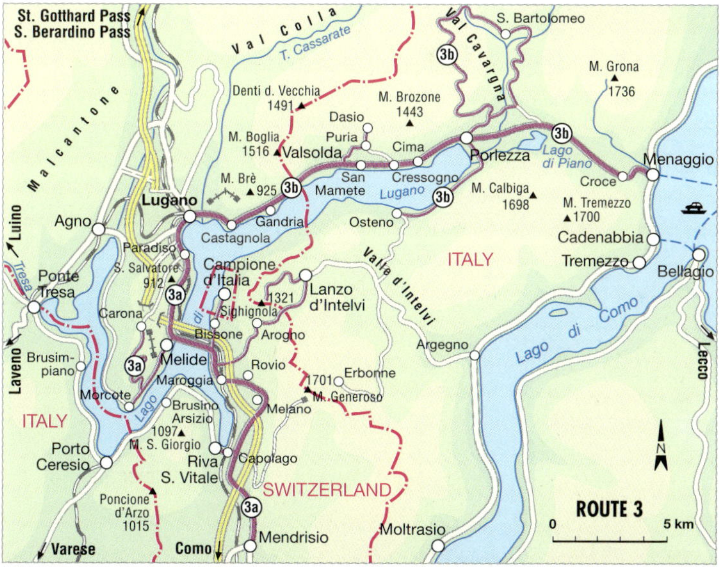

chapels in the 18th century and much interior renovation. The ★ Renaissance facade (1500–17) is a very attractive sight with its three portals, richly carved figures and round window, and is considered one of the finest examples of Lombard Renaissance architecture in all Ticino.

Villa Favorita

Don't miss the city's museums either, especially the **Museo Cantonale d'Arte** (Palazzo Reali, Via Canova 10, Wednesday to Sunday 10am–5pm, Tuesday 2–5pm) and the Museo Cantonale di Storia Naturale. Until a short time ago, the Thyssen-Bornemisza collection of paintings in the famous **Villa Favorita** in Castagnola was a must for all art lovers, but in 1992 it was transferred to Madrid. Now the villa contains works by 19th- and 20th-century American and European artists.

Morcote

Melide is a popular holiday resort with a special attraction: the 1:25 scale models collectively known as ★ **Swiss Miniature** (9am–7pm; July and August 9am–10pm), representing the most important sights of Switzerland (towns, buildings, etc).

A cable railway leads up from the lake to ★ **Carona**, a picturesque mountain village with several attractive churches. From here it's possible to hike along the mountain to the next destination on the route, the village of ★★ **Morcote**, one of the most popular excursion destinations in the region. Even though it was discovered by the tourist industry quite early on, Morcote has successfully retained much of its historic substance. The village blends in harmoniously with its surroundings, and this has made it a magnet for visitors. A flight of steps laid out in 1732 leads up to the terraced cemetery and the parish church of ★ **Santa Maria del Sasso**, built in the 13th century; inside there are several magnificent Renaissance frescoes. The free-standing campanile dates from 1539.

Swiss Miniature

Near the village of **Bissone** is the Ponte Diga, built in 1844, which takes rail and road traffic across the narrowest part of the lake. Bissone is famous as the home of several famous families of artists such as Borromini, Maderno and Tencalla. Its most famous son was the architect Francesco Borromini (1599–1667), the biggest rival of Gian Lorenzo Bernini in Rome. Bissone does not possess even one of the master's works, however.

At the southern end of Lake Lugano is **Capolago**, which used to be an important trading centre before the Gotthard railway was built, and was fortified by the Visconti. It is the birthplace of architect Carlo Maderna (1556–1629), who built the facade of St Peter's in Rome. Capolago is the starting-point for tours to ★★ **Monte Generoso** (1,701m/5,580ft); in good weather the mountain panorama from the top extends from Monte Viso (3,841m/12,600ft) to the Bernina (4,049m/13,280ft). Early summer, when the flowers are all in bloom, is the best time to take the rack railway to the top.

Creeper in Riva San Vitale

The small town of **Riva San Vitale** (pop. 2,000) is most famous for its Early Christian baptistery and the domed church of Santa Croce. Inhabited as long ago as prehistoric times, and first mentioned as *Sobenno* in 774, during medieval times Riva San Vitale was one of Como's bases in its war against Milan. The town is dominated by the mighty dome of ★★ **Santa Croce**, one of the finest churches in Switzerland. It was built between 1588 and 1592 by the architect Giovanni Antonio Piotto, from Vacallo in the Mendrisiotto. Despite sharing several characteristics with contemporary centralised structures (e.g. Todi, Montepulciano), the building also presages the baroque era. Eight mighty columns support the huge dome crowned with its lantern. The fresco decoration, with its many strange figures and gargoyle-like Mannerist faces, is also very impressive.

Riva San Vitale's second claim to fame is its ★★ **Baptistery of San Giovanni**, beside the parish church of San Vitale. The centralised structure with its octagonal cupola was built in around 500, and originally had a square ambulatory (some parts of the original roof still survive in the western wall). The eastern apse probably dates from the Carolingian period; the fresco remains showing the *Crucifixion* have been dated to around 1000; and the paintings in the niches to the left and right of the apse date from the 14th and 15th centuries. Sections of the artistically paved marble floor also survive; the octagonal *piscina* in the pavement was originally used for total-immersion baptisms before the erection of the enormous baptism stone (2m/7ft across). The municipal museum in Riva also

San Giovanni

Cosma e Damiano in Mendrisio

contains an interesting exhibition of works by the 19th-century 'mountain painter' Giovanni Segantini.

From Riva, continue to **Mendrisio** (pop. 7,000), a lively town which has retained its old *Borgo*, several churches and numerous palazzi despite a lot of busy construction work. The Easter processions here are famed far beyond the borders of Ticino, and are a very colourful affair. The old town centre is dominated by the parish church of **SS Cosma e Damiano**, a monumental centralised structure dating from the 19th century with an octagonal dome. The former monastery church of San Giovanni Battista was built above a previous structure between 1722 and 1738; it contains some marvellous stucco and also several *trompe l'oeil* ceiling paintings. Mendrisio also possesses one of the most magnificent baroque palazzi in Ticino: the **Palazzo Pollini** (1719–21).

From Mendrisio it's only a short distance to Como, and the end of the trip.

Route 3b: Lugano to Menaggio

Lugano – Gandria –Porlezza – Menaggio (28km/17 miles) *See map, p29*

This route leads from Lugano via the very picturesque village of Gandria to Menaggio on Lake Como. The route goes through regions that are not only very scenic but have also produced several fine artists and architects over the centuries.

Gandria promenade

Leave Lugano along the road to Porlezza, which follows a steep section beyond Castagnola with fine views across the lake and the Sighignola Massif. Along this section of road it's actually quite easy to miss ★ **Gandria**, which lies just below the route. This much-visited village is a jumble of houses on a steep slope right beside the lake, and is very picturesque, especially when viewed from the water. It can be reached on foot from Castagnola (1hr) along a path lined with subtropical vegetation. On the opposite bank is the Cantine di Gandria landing stage. Here the original **Museo Doganale** or Customs Museum (Easter to mid-October daily 1.30–5.30pm), is worth a brief visit; it contains a fascinating selection of smuggled goods of all kinds.

Beyond Gandria the route crosses the Italian border. The hamlet of San Mamete marks the entrance to the picturesque ★ **Valsolda**, a long valley surrounded by high Dolomite peaks which is very popular with hikers and climbers. The small village of **Puria** was the birthplace of the most important artist-architect of the Lombard Renaissance, Pellegrino Tibaldi (1527–96). He worked in this region and also in Rome and Milan, but his career took off properly when he worked for Philip II in Madrid. Valsolda was also the home of the Italian author Antonio Fogazzaro (1842–1911), whose novel *Piccolo Mondo Antico* is set in this region. The majestic mountains and the lake provide an atmospheric backdrop for the ★ **Santuario della Madonna della Caravina**, a magnificent baroque structure built in 1663, and situated above the main road between Cressogno and Cima.

A fine backdrop…

…and perfect views

The town of **Porlezza** (pop. 3,800) marks the eastern end of Lake Lugano. It dates back to prehistoric times, and during the Roman era was the port of *Raetia*. Later on this fishing town, like so many others between Lakes Maggiore and Como, was the home of several generations of artists, including the Sanmichele and Della Porta families. Guglielmo della Porta was a pupil of Michelangelo, and is famous for his work on the dome of St Peter's in Rome after his master's death in 1564. Unfortunately Porlezza has no important artistic monuments of its own. The parish church of **San Vittore** (17th-century with fresco decoration) is worth a visit, as is the Romanesque campanile of the ruined church of San Maurizio, far outside the town at the foot of the Monte Calbiga (1,698m/5,570ft). The church marks the site of the former Porlezza, which was destroyed in a landslide. Remains of an early medieval settlement were discovered during archaeological excavations in the area.

There are several good excursions from Porlezza. Try visiting **Osteno** on the southern shore of Lake Lugano, with its attractive church; inside there is an astounding marble ★ *Madonna and Child* by Andrea Bregno, dated 1464.

Halfway between Porlezza and Osteno the road leads past the entrance to the **Grotte di Resci**a, a small limestone cavern.

Not far away from Porlezza is the ★ **Val Cavargna**, a picturesque mountain region with several pretty villages, magnificent chestnut groves and beech forests, a profusion of wild flowers and numerous walking and hiking routes. One well-surfaced route connects Porlezza with both the Val Cavargna and the **Val Rezzo**, and a 30-km (18-mile) round trip by car affords several magnificent views of the region. Note the abandoned mountain hamlets, however: the problem of depopulation is affecting many of these Southern Alpine valleys.

Several more marked routes lead from Buggiolo (1,035m/3,400ft) to the Passo di San Lucio (1,548m/5,050ft; 2hrs), an ancient way of gaining access to the Val Colla in Ticino, and along the ridge of the Monte Garzirola (2,116m/6,940ft; 2hrs from San Lucio), which is famed for its magnificent panoramic views.

Passing glance

The road to Menaggio leads past the small and shallow Lago di Piano, which has a maximum depth of around 5m (16ft) and was once a part of Lake Lugano. Towering above the vineyards of Carlazzo here is the high rocky peak of **Monte Grona** (1,736m/5,695ft), and across to the right is the forest-covered northern flank of **Monte Tremezzo** (1,700m/5,570ft).

At the tiny hamlet of Croce, the road begins its winding descent to the western bank of Lake Como, with some good views of Ballagio and the mountains around the Valsassina. One particularly good view of the lake and its mountain backdrop can be enjoyed from the **Crocetta a Specchi** (505m/1,650ft), easily and quickly reached from Croce; it takes around an hour to climb the Sasso di San Martino (862m/2,820ft), where a magnificent panorama meets the eye, extending northeast as far as the granite peaks of the Bergell.

Menaggio fishmonger

The town of **Menaggio** (pop. 3,200) lies on a small promontory at the point where the Val Sanagra meets Lake Como. This is also where the important connecting route with Lugano branches off, resulting in chaotic traffic conditions (particularly in the summer). The area slightly inland, with its hiking routes and excursion destinations, is far more peaceful and attractive. A winding road leads north to Plesio and on to **Breglia**, with its little Madonna di Breglia church, visible from afar, and also the observation point known as the Belvedere San Domenico (820m/2,690ft). From Breglia, hikers can follow the path to the **Rifugio Menaggio** (superb views of Lake Como) and from there continue to the summit of Monte Grona.

Route 4

★★ Como

The city of ★★ **Como** (pop. 95,000) has two distinct faces: the noble one, facing the lake, and the ugly one that extends into the Brianza. The best direction to approach Como from is north, either across the lake or along one of the lakeside roads. This is when the town is at its most magical: green, grey and a soft ochre, bathed in Mediterranean light, the walls of the old town retain a sobriety that is distinctly Lombard. From this angle it's impossible to see behind the noble facade and into Como's industrial heart. The first craftsmen to make the town famous were the architects and stonemasons from the region, known as *Maestri Comacini*, who built such magnificent Lombard architecture; and the town's industrial future was secured by the introduction of silk manufacturing in 1510 by Pietro Boldoni. *Pura seta di Como* is a phrase often heard internationally nowadays, and the silk industry of this region accounts for almost one quarter of world production: every day Como produces the equivalent of 250km (155 miles) of silk ribbon!

Como Cathedral: carving detail

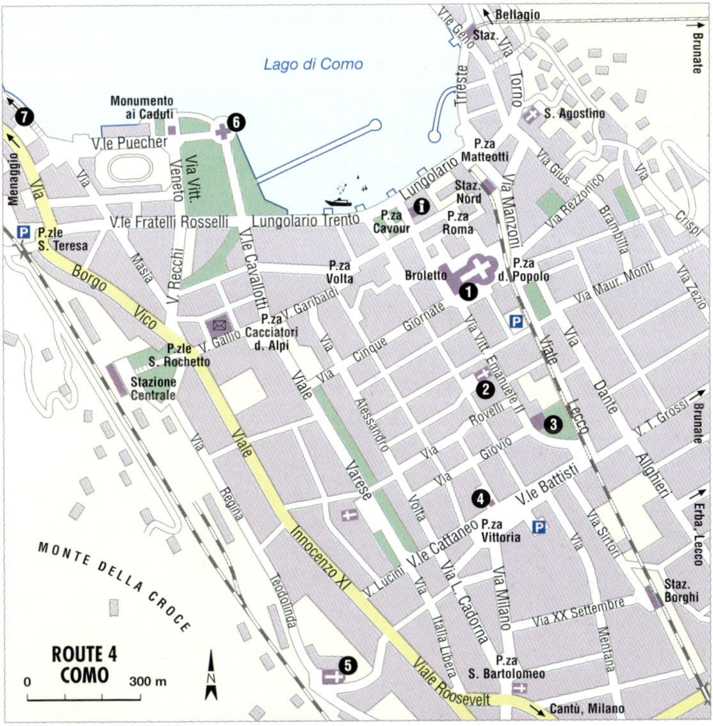

History

Growing up in Como

Though inhabited long before the Romans arrived, Como is most famous historically as the birthplace of Pliny the Elder (AD24–79), compiler of the 37-volume *Naturalis Historia*, and of his nephew Pliny the Younger (AD62–113). The Romans were followed by Lombards and Franks, and during the Middle Ages Como suffered from several battles between the Guelphs (pro-papacy) and the Ghibellines (pro-empire). During the Ten Years' War with Milan (1118–27) the town was partially destroyed, but managed to recover largely because of support from the emperor Barbarossa. From 1335 Como was ruled by the Visconti, and from 1450 by the Sforza, and flourished culturally as a result – in contrast to Spanish rule, which lasted until 1714. Economic recovery only really began under the Austrian Habsburgs, and the silk industry in particular made Como quite prosperous again. Today the old town of Como – the *città murata* – is largely closed to motor traffic, and its layout is almost identical to that of the original Roman *castrum* on the site. For some time now there has been a complete ban on new construction; restoration is the order of the day. Como's ancient walls and arcades are ideal for a stroll back into the centuries, and the gourmet specialities and exclusive fashions make shopping here a very memorable experience.

Cathedral interior

City Tour

The best place to start a tour of the historic old town is the cathedral square, in which the ★★ **Cathedral** ❶, the **Broletto** (former town hall, built in 1215) and the **Torre del Comune** (old city tower) make up a harmonious and grandiose architectural ensemble. Both the Torre del Comune and the Broletto, with its Tuscan-style black-and-

Refreshment on the piazza

white patterned facade, date from the early 13th century; the cathedral was begun somewhat later, in 1396, and construction work continued – with the odd interruption – right into the 18th century. The 75-m (245-ft) high dome above the crossing, for instance, was built in 1744 by the Turin architect Juvara. Nevertheless, the building as a whole is exceptionally harmonious. Lorenzo degli Spagli's original design was Gothic; the ★ facade, begun in 1457, is considered a masterpiece of Early Lombard Renaissance architecture. Much of its statuary is by the Rodari brothers, e.g. the *Adoration of the Magi* relief in the lunette, and the two seated figures placed proudly on either side of the main portal, Pliny the Elder and Pliny the Younger. Tommaso and Jacopo Rodari also did the so-called Porta della Rana or 'Frog Portal' on the northern side of the cathedral, which owes its name to a rather sketchy relief of a frog.

Looking towards the altar

The interior of the cathedral is rather dark, but it contains several artistic masterpieces including the enormous 16th-century Tuscan and Flemish tapestries lining the nave, a fine *Deposition* by Tommaso Rodari in the left transept, and several altar paintings by the great Bernardino Luini (*Adoration of the Magi*) and also Gaudenzio Ferrari (*Flight from Egypt*).

Just a few short steps away from the cathedral is the church of ★ **San Fedele** ❷, a Romanesque basilica built above the ruins of a previous Carolingian structure on the site during the 12th century. The apse with its dwarf gallery and the trefoil ground-plan are both reminiscent of Charlemagne's Palatine Chapel in Aachen. The northern portal has some very fine sculpture work, and inside to the left of the northern apse there are several frescoes dating from the 12th and 13th centuries, thematically related to the ones in the baptistery of Riva San Vitale (*see page 31*).

Museum vase

The Palazzo Giovio houses the ★ **Museo Archeologico Artistico** ❸ (Tuesday to Saturday 9.30am–12.30pm and 2–5pm, Sunday 10am–1pm), one of Como's two municipal museums. The oldest finds here date from around 8000BC, and there are also several fascinating Roman, Romanesque and Gothic exhibits. The **picture gallery** documents Lombard art of the 16th to 18th centuries, and there is also an exotic section displaying art from the various Mediterranean cultures. The other museum, the **Museo del Risorgimento G Garibaldi** (Tuesday to Saturday 9.30am–12.30pm and 2–5pm, Sunday 10am–1pm), inside the neoclassical Palazzo Olginati next door to the Palazzo Giovio, has some interesting exhibits documenting the town's history, its 19th-century liberation struggles and the two World Wars.

Lombard painting in the gallery

Family outing

One of the most majestic gates still surviving from Como's medieval fortifications is the mighty **Torre di Porta Vittoria** ❹, a full 40m (130ft) high, with its over-sized double windows. From the Piazza Vittoria it's not far to the church of ★★ **Sant'Abbondio** ❺ which, despite its location between the railway line and some ugly industrial buildings, is one of the most important Early Lombard Romanesque structures in Italy. The five-aisled basilica with its two bell-towers has several stylistic features in common with structures north of the Alps (e.g. Speyer Cathedral in Germany). The strikingly large choir contains Gothic frescoes dating from around 1350, and the ★ cloister to the north of the building, with its twin-storeyed arcade, was added in the 16th century.

Tempting cakes in Como

There's a good view of the town and the lake from the **Castello Baradello** (access via the Piazza San Rocco), a picturesque ruined fort on the eastern slopes of the Monte della Croce (536m/1,760ft). Out on the western side of the harbour is the neoclassical structure known as the **Tempio Voltano** ❻ (daily except Monday 10am–noon and 3–6pm, October to March 2–4pm), dedicated to the famous physicist and discoverer Alessandro Volta (1745–1827), after whom the electrical unit *volt* is named; his personal effects and also the batteries he invented are on display here.

Youth Hostel at Villa dell'Olmo

The western lake promenade leads from the Piazza Cavour past several attractive neoclassical villas to the ★ **Villa dell'Olmo** ❼, a magnificent estate laid out between 1782 and 1787. Its first important visitor was Napoleon, who arrived here just after the building was completed with his wife Josephine. The Villa dell'Olmo is by far the most majestic of the neoclassical villas in this part of Como.

Route 5

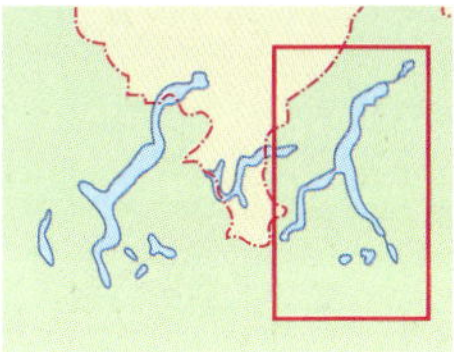

★★ Lake Como

Over the centuries the splendid countryside around Lake Como has been gradually made even more attractive by the hand of man, and it is probably true to say that this lake, known to the Romans as *Lacus Lario*, is the most impressive of the Upper Italian lakes. Not only Como Cathedral but also the rows of magnificent villas with beautiful gardens along the edge of the lake all testify to the wonderfully harmonious blend of natural scenery and architecture in this part of the world. Like a fjord, Lake Como is surrounded by steep mountains. Unlike Lake Maggiore

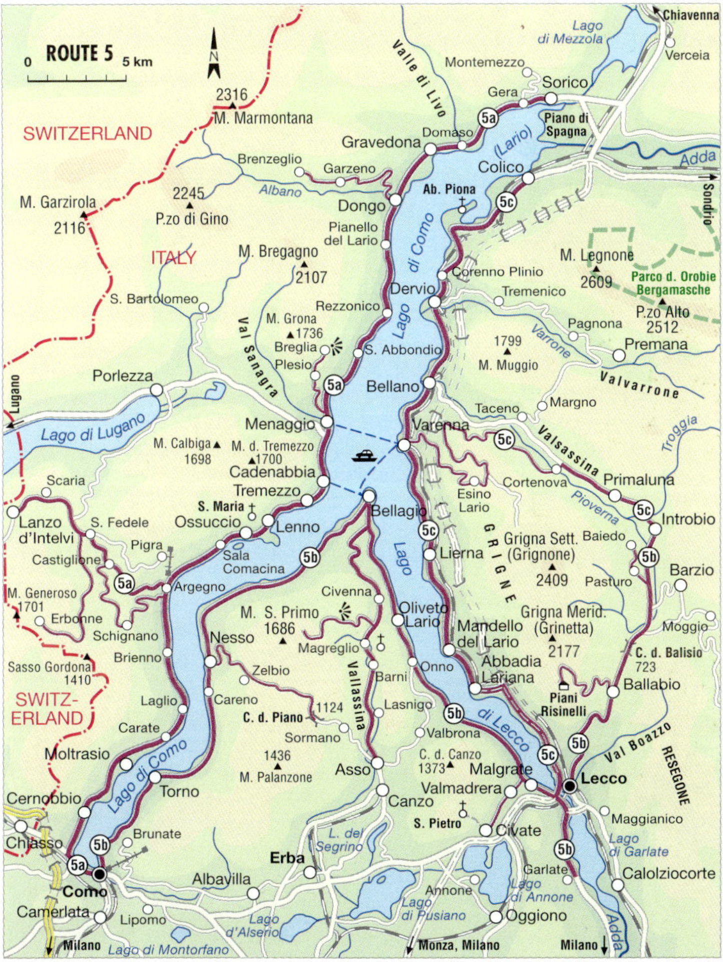

it does not extend across a plain; it is an Alpine lake, despite its Mediterranean vegetation, and southern-baroque style villas and parks. But this contrast is what makes the *Lario*, as it is called locally, so attractive. Even though a surface area of 146sq km (56sq miles) makes it only the third-largest lake in Upper Italy, with its depth of 410m (1,350ft) it is the deepest inland lake in Europe. Lake Como is roughly 50km (32 miles) long and 4.5km (3 miles) across at its widest point. It is unusually-shaped, reminding most people of an upside-down 'Y'. The main rivers flowing into the lake are the Mera, which descends from the Bergell, and the Adda, which has its source in the Bernina Massif, leaves the lake near Lecco and finally joins the Po not far from Cremona.

The high, rocky peaks to the east of Lake Como certainly provide the most impressive view, but the western shore, too, has several delights of its own a little further inland.

Guests at the Villa d'Este

5a – The Western Shore

Cernobbio – Tremezzo – Menaggio – Gravedona – Sorico (59km/37 miles) *See map, p39*

The route up the lake from Como first arrives at **Cernobbio** (pop. 8,000), where the **Villa d'Este** begins the long line of famous residences along the lake's western shore. Built between 1565–70 by Pellegrino Tibaldi, the villa was altered in the early 19th century by Caroline of Brunswick in accordance with contemporary taste. Today the Villa d'Este is a luxury hotel and open only to guests.

Pass the magnificent gardens and villas to reach **Carate**, where the small 11th-century church of Santa Maria is just a short distance above the main road. The Romanesque

A sedate form of recreation

campanile, 15th-century frescoes and fine view of the lake all form a very memorable ensemble.

The small town of **Argegno** is a good starting-point for a detour into the ★ **Intelvi Valley**, a high plateau with some delightful landscape, but famed above all for producing a whole host of painters, architects and stonemasons. These *Maestri Antelami* not only influenced Lombard art for decades but were active all over Europe and even the Near East. Several of these masters have also left traces here in the Valle d'Intelvi: in **Scaria**, for instance, which has superb stucco work by Diego Carlone and frescoes by Carlo Carlone. Keep your eyes open in this valley – there are several artistic and architectural discoveries to be made. The Valle d'Intelvi is a paradise for nature-lovers too, however; its unique location between Lake Lugano and Lake Como provides a whole series of magnificent panoramic views to accompany hikes. One particularly impressive peak for climbers to head for here is the **Sassa Gordona** (1,410m/4,625ft).

Just before Sala Comacina, the only island in Lake Como comes into view, the **Isola Comacina**. Around 600m (640yds) long and up to 200m (220yds) wide, the island was more important historically than it is today. It was settled during Roman times, and during the Middle Ages there were five churches on it at one point. In 1169 the settlement on the island was wiped out by Como in retaliation for its pact with Milan during the Ten Years' War (1118–27). All that remains today of the original town are the ruined walls of the Romanesque basilica of Sant'Eufemia.

At the entrance to the Val Perlana is **Ossuccio** (pop. 1,500), where the simple church of Santa Maria Maddalena has an unusual campanile with a brick belfry, dating from the 14th century. Above the village is a 17th-century Via Crucis with 14 chapels, and higher still, the basilica of ★ **San Benedetto** in the Val Perlana is probably the finest of the Romanesque churches on the lake. **Lenno** also has an interesting church: **Santo Stefano**, though much renovated during the 16th century, is originally Lombard. The crypt was part of an 11th-century basilica, and remains of a Roman bath have been discovered beneath the church. Santo Stefano's octagonal baptistery also dates from the 11th century.

Further along the route, **Mezzegra** comes into view. The place is famous for one reason: it was here on 28 April 1945, one day after having been taken prisoner in nearby Dongo while trying to flee to Switzerland, that Benito Mussolini and his mistress Clara Petacci were shot dead.

Uphill struggle in the Intelvi Valley

Scaria parish church

Isola Comacina: coffee ceremony

Ossuccio fisherman

Villa Carlotta

The two resorts of ★ **Tremezzo** (pop. 1,300) and **Cadenabbia** are almost always busy, especially in the area round the ★★★ **Villa Carlotta** (daily March to October), the most famous and the most lavishly decorative villa on Lake Como. Innumerable visitors come here each year to marvel at the magnificent ★ terraced garden, the elegant rooms (e.g. the great marble hall), the sculpture and painting collection (including works by Canova and Thorvaldsen) and the fine view across the lake to the Bellagio peninsula and the grey rocks of the Grigna. The Villa Carlotta was originally built in the baroque style (1747), and received its present neoclassical appearance at the beginning of the 19th century. It was sold to Princess Mary of Prussia in 1856, and she bequeathed it to her daughter Charlotte. No trip to the Lake Como region is complete without a visit to this superb building.

The route now continues on to **Menaggio** (*see Route 3, page 34*), beyond which the landscape gradually begins to get starker, and generally more Alpine than Mediterranean. Snowy mountain peaks start appearing; the northern end of the *Lario* is only around 40km (24 miles) away from the main Alpine range. The lakeshore road leads through Sant'Abbondio, Rezzonico and the collection of communities making up Pianello del Lario. There's a good ★ **boat museum** (daily July to mid-September) in the community of Calozzo, where many of the various boat types used on the lakes are exhibited, including gondolas, fishing boats and punts.

Gravedona: Palazzo Gallio

The historic centre of the upper part of Lake Como is ★ **Gravedona** (pop. 3,000), an independent commune during medieval times which later became famous for its goldsmiths. Right next to the lake is the **Palazzo Gallio**, built in 1583 according to designs by Pellegrino Tibaldi, on the site of a ruined fort that was destroyed during the Milan-Como war of 1118–27. Don't miss the church of ★ **Santa Maria del Tiglio** on the south side of the town: it is one of the most important Romanesque churches on Lake Como, and was originally an Early Christian baptistery (remains of mosaics and font). The facade is dominated by the tall, octagonal tower, and inside, a monumental 13th-century statue of Christ opens his arms in welcome. The neighbouring church of San Vicenzo dates from the 11th century, but was altered completely (apart from the crypt) during the 17th and 18th centuries.

Gravedona is dominated by the church of **Santa Maria delle Grazie**, built in 1467 as part of an Augustinian monastery. It contains important frescoes by 15th- and 16th-century Lombard artists. A word of warning, though: the place is hardly ever open!

Torno

5b – Como to Lecco via Bellagio

Como – Bellagio – Lecco (52km/32 miles) *See map, p39*

The trips to Bellagio, the 'Pearl of the Lake', and to Lecco are both breathtaking, and if you combine them with detours into the higher regions between the two arms of the lake – Monte San Primo, for instance (1,686m/5,530ft), or at least the Madonna del Ghisallo observation point (755m/2,450ft), the experience is unforgettable. The best views are of course to be had at Bellagio, the most famous resort on the lake; it is uniquely situated and still has an unmistakeable charm of its own, even in these days of heavy traffic and mass tourism. Approaching Bellagio by steamer from Como is an unforgettable experience. The roads along the lakeshore are very quiet in contrast, and that's not only because of all their hairpins. The villages along the steep shores are sleepy and picturesque, set against the blue backdrop of the lake, and there are far more old buildings than new ones. To really enjoy this route, allow two days and spend the night in Bellagio; those with less time will have to make do with one day.

There are several villas between Como and **Torno**, among them the magnificent ★ **Pliniana** – which, by the way, has nothing to do with either Pliny the Elder or the Younger. The Pliniana was built in 1575 by Pellegrino Tibaldi, the architect who designed the villa for Como's governor Giovanni Anguissola. History books mention the count's involvement in the murder of Duke Pier Luigi Farnese (a son of Pope Paul III and one of the most evil men of the Renaissance). The villa had several changes of owner after that, but also many illustrious guests, including Byron, Stendhal, Napoleon, Liszt and Rossini – who wrote his opera *Tancredi* here in just six days. The villa is not open to the public.

The route to Bellagio: Nesso

Boating on a blue lake

Bellagio bathers and the approach to Villa Melzi

The old part of Torno has several picturesque corners. The church of **San Giovanni** is Romanesque in origin (12th-century campanile), and was extended in the 15th century. Note the Early Christian tombstone in the nave.

The views get better and better as you continue towards Bellagio. One very pretty village is Careno, part of the municipality of **Nesso** (pop. 1,700), where the houses almost seem to be above rather than next to each other. Above Careno is the entrance to the **Grotta Masera**, one of several caverns in this region. Up on the **Colma del Piano** (1,124m/3,687ft), 12km (7 miles) from Nesso, there is a magnificent view across the valleys and mountains surrounding Asso and Canzo.

The town of ★★★ **Bellagio** (pop. 4,000) really lives up to its name. Its dramatic location at the point where Lake Como and Lake Lecco divide combines with the panorama, the villas and the gardens to produce a truly admirable work of man. The Romans called it *Bilacus* ('between the lakes'). The promontory is approached in real style by ship, and it becomes clear why Flaubert wrote *on voudrait vivre ici et y mourir* when he first caught sight of Bellagio.

The tiny Borgo lies on the western side of the narrow peninsula. Narrow flights of steps lead up from the lake promenade to the parish church of **San Giacomo**. This three-aisled Romanesque structure with its 17th-century tower contains a very expressive *Entombment* attributed to Perugino (c. 1500).

But what would Bellagio be without its villas and its ★★ parks? Some of them have a very varied history, such as the one surrounding the **Villa Giulia** on the eastern side of the peninsula, formerly the residence of Belgian king

Leopold I and today in private hands. On the hill above the town is the ★ **Villa Serbelloni** (guided tours daily 10am–4pm), originally Renaissance but with neoclassical additions. One of the two villas owned by Pliny the Younger formerly stood on this site; later on it was converted into a Lombard fortress.

The entrance to the second large park in Ballagio, the one surrounding the ★ **Villa Melzi**, is in the suburb of Loppia on the road to Como. The cool, neoclassical villa was built in 1815, and the park (9am–6pm), dotted with statues, has a marvellous collection of exotic plants (avenues of plane trees, azaleas, alpine roses). Another very romantic place is the **Buco dei Carpi**, a cavern down by the lake 5km (3 miles) out of Bellagio in the direction of Como, with very attractive light effects reminiscent of the Blue Grotto on Capri.

Azaleas line the waterfront

Alongside its villas and parks Bellagio also has mountains, and the somewhat steep and rocky hinterland is ideal for hikes and excursions. Try a drive up to the **Madonna del Ghisallo** (755m/2,477ft) via **Civenna**, a delightful resort above the eastern arm of the Lario. The best place for a view in the triangle formed by Como, Lecco and Bellagio (Traigola Lariano) is the ★ **Monte San Primo** (1,686m/5,530ft), which offers a breathtaking panorama. The path to the summit can be reached by driving south from Bellagio and turning right in Guello.

Continue onwards now via Malgrate to reach **Lecco** (pop. 51,000), with its smoking factory chimneys and traffic chaos. Very little remains of its former beauty these days. Nevertheless, Lecco is definitely worth a visit, not least because it is the setting of one of the most famous books in the world: *I promessi sposi* (*The Betrothed*) by Italy's greatest Romantic novelist, Alessandro Manzoni (1785–1873). Written in 1827, the book had immense patriotic appeal for Italians of the nationalistic Risorgimento period, and is a sympathetic portrayal of the struggle of two peasant lovers to marry in the face of opposition from a vicious local landowner and the local parish priest.

Manzoni in Lecco

Lecco has several interesting sights. At the southwestern corner of the central square is the battlemented **Torre del Castello**, part of a former 15th-century Visconti fortress, and housing the **Museo del Risorgimento e della Resistenza**. The nearby **Ponte Azzone Visconti** also dates back to the days of the Visconti (1336–38). In the suburb of Caleotti, the 18th-century neoclassical **Villa Manzoni** is where the famous author (*see above*) spent his youth. The 18th-century **Palazzo Belgioioso** contains the **Natural History Museum**, which has several fascinating prehistoric and Roman exhibits from the region, including a valuable relief dating from the 1st century BC.

Palazzo Belgioioso

Lecco's impressive surroundings

Culture vulture

Lecco is indisputably ugly, but the scenery surrounding it is not. The lake and the mountains are quite magnificent, and ideal for excursions. One hour's walk away from the village of **Civate** is the church of ★★ **San Pietro al Monte** (639m/2,100ft). Why a Benedictine monastery was founded here in this remote mountain region during the 8th century is not known, but the architecture blends in very harmoniously with the scenery. Originally San Pietro was a hall church with an eastern apse; during the 11th century the entrance was switched to the eastern end to create direct access to the Oratorio San Benedetto, a centralised Romanesque structure situated further down. San Pietro's main claim to fame is its stucco and frescoes dating from the late 11th century, revealing the influence of Byzantine artists. The lunette fresco showing angels fighting a seven-headed dragon is very fine, as is the stucco work on the baldachin. The crypt contains further reliefs and frescoes.

★ The **Grigna** is the vast limestone massif next to Lecco, between the eastern shore of Lake Como and the Valsassina, and its highest points are the Grignone (2,409m/7,900ft) and the Grignetta (2,177m/7,140ft), both of them with a vast choice of hiking possibilities. The southern Grigna is particularly reminiscent of the Dolomites; an interesting 3-hr route – for experienced climbers only – connects it with the Grignone.

5c – The Eastern Shore

Lecco – Lierna – Varenna – Colico (41km/25 miles) *See map, p39*

The stretch along the eastern shore of Lake Como can easily be covered in half an hour, thanks to the new highway. Although the trip does give an idea of the sheer length of this relic from the Ice Age, lying like an 'Alpine fjord' between its steep shores, to get to know the lake and its hinterland allow one day to follow this route

The first town on the eastern shore of the Lago di Lecco – the name given to the eastern arm of Lake Como – is **Abbadia Lariana** (pop. 2,200), 7km (4 miles) outside Lecco. The name refers to a long-vanished Benedictine monastery; the oldest traces of settlement date back to pre-Roman times. Most of the older buildings can be found in the upper part of the town, and there's a good view from the **Monte di Borbino** (486m/1,600ft), a 30-min walk from the town centre. Abbadia Lariana's old silk factory, built in 1919, has now been turned into a small museum; the highlight here is an enormous water-driven silk-spinning machine with 432 bobbins.

The main reason the town of **Mandello del Lario** (pop. 9,500) became famous is because of motor bikes – produced by the firm of Guzzi (founded in 1921). The bikes have been successful for decades in races all over the world. Apart from all that horsepower, Mandello also has several cultural-historical attractions: the parish church of **San Lorenzo** (9th, 12th and 17th-century), several old arcaded townhouses and also the richly-decorated church of **Madonna del Fiume**, one of the most successful baroque buildings in the region. The smaller, 15th-century church of **San Nicolò** has a number of interesting late medieval features, both inside and out.

Further on, **Lierna** (pop. 1,500) is a very old area of settlement: finds dating from the Bronze Age and the foundations of a Roman villa have been discovered here. The small church in the suburb of Castello used to be part of a medieval castle. It's worth stopping briefly to admire the shortest river in Italy: the Fiumelatte, or 'milk stream', just outside Varenna. From its source to the lake it covers a total distance of 250m (820ft), and this earned it a mention in Leonardo da Vinci's *Codice Atlantico*. Because of a geological phenomenon, its milky waters only flow between spring and autumn.

Vertigo in Varenna

At the widest part of the lake (4.5km/3 miles) lies the small town of ★ **Varenna** (pop. 1,000), with its picturesque centre of piled-up houses intersected by narrow alleys and dominated by the tower of the parish church of San Giorgio. The basilica dates from around 1300, but underwent several alterations in the 17th and 18th centuries. There is a noteworthy *Baptism of Christ* (1553) altar painting here by Sigismondo de Magistris. Just outside the town is the **Villa Monastero** (April to October 9.30am–noon

Villa Monastero: the grounds

Villa Monastero: detail

and 2.30–6pm) with its magnificent grounds. The building was originally a convent, founded by the Cistercians in 1208 for nuns who had been evicted from Isola Comacina, and dissolved in 1567 because of the reputation of promiscuity gained by their successors. After several changes of ownership the villa is now a science centre owned by the Italian state.

Don't miss a detour from Varenna to ★ **Esino Lario** (pop. 800). Situated at the top of a steep and winding road, this small town of many villas is sometimes known as the 'Pearl of the Grigna'. From the parish church there's a view westwards as far as Lake Lugano, and the peaks of the Grigna can be seen to the southeast. The **Museo della Grigna** contains some fascinating local finds (July and August daily 9am–noon and 4–7pm). Another excursion from Varenna goes via the 'Panoramica del Lario', and leads into the **Valsassina**, a magnificent southern Alpine valley much favoured by the Ancient Romans.

Valsassina Valley

Continue now to **Bellano** (pop. 4,500). The 14th-century black-and-white striped facade and rose window of the parish church of SS Nazaro e Celso are worthy of note, but the real tourist attraction here is the *orrido*, a wildly romantic and very steep gorge (only recommended for those with a head for heights) just outside the town.

Striving for perfection

Not far away from the relatively uninteresting industrial town of **Dervio** (pop. 2,400) is the picturesque little village of ★ **Corenno Plinio**, which is said to derive its name from its early settlers who came from Corinth and from Pliny the Elder who gave the site his highest praise. The village church, ruined fortifications and pretty old houses are all huddled together attractively on a small rise next to the lake.

A bit further along, romantically situated on a peninsula, is ★ **Piona Abbey**. It was founded as long ago as the 7th century, but the existing buildings are of far later origin: San Nicolò was consecrated in 1138, and its magnificent cloister dates from the 13th century. Today the abbey is occupied by Cistercians who not only lead an exemplary life on their idyllic island but also produce a delicious liqueur.

The northernmost town on the eastern shore of Lake Como is **Colico** (pop. 5,000). The rough mountains round about lend it an almost Alpine appearance, and the ruins of the old fortress up on the **Montecchio** to the northeast of Colico blend in with the landscape. Originally built by the Spanish at the beginning of the 17th century, the fortress was destroyed in 1798 by the French.

Route 6

★★ Bergamo

Bergamo, known as *Bergomum* to the Romans, consists of two sections: the 'upper town' *(alta)*, which is the oldest part, and the more modern lower section *(bassa* or *piana)*. It was originally a settlement of the Celtic tribe of the *Orobi*, but became a Roman town in 196BC. After its destruction at the hands of Attila the Hun it became the seat of a Lombard duchy, and by the 12th century the town had become an independent commune. From 1329 onwards the Visconti family ruled, but in 1428 it became Venetian property, remaining so until 1797 when the French took control and included it in Napoleon's Cisalpine Republic. Bergamo owes much of its architectural and artistic beauty to the long years of Venetian rule. In 1815 the city became Austrian, and remained so until 1859 when it became part of the Kingdom of Italy.

Palazzo della Ragione

City Tour

The two parts of the city are linked by a rack railway. The older, upper part is closed to traffic, and the best place to begin a stroll through is the **Piazza Vecchia** ❶. Note the Venetian lions on the **Contarini Fountain** in the middle, erected in 1780 during the final years of Venetian rule by Mayor Contarini. It's worth going up the Torre del Comune for a very rewarding view. Continue now from the Piazza Vecchia to the Piazza del Duomo, or Cathedral Square. Bergamo's Romanesque cathedral was rebuilt

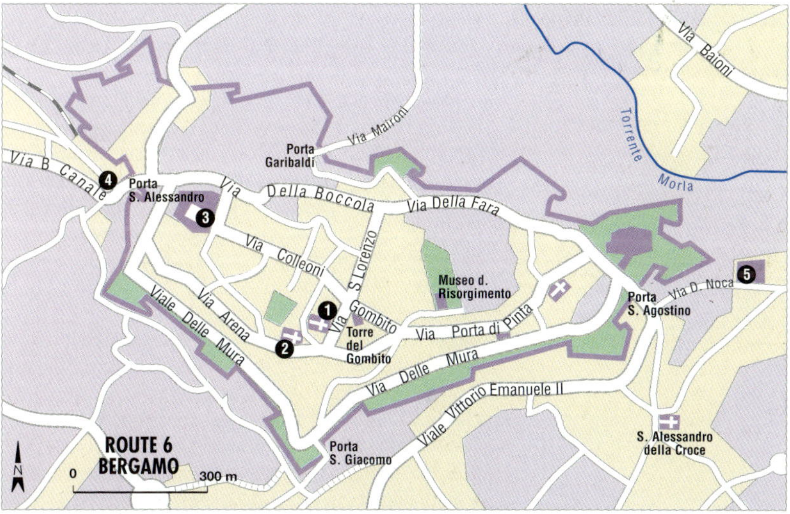

in 1483 and 1639; its white facade is almost completely hidden from view by the buildings surrounding it. Despite its simple beauty, the Duomo is however completely upstaged by the adjacent 12th-century basilica of ★ **Santa Maria Maggiore** ❷, begun in 1137 and rebuilt during the 14th and 15th centuries. The red-and-white marble porch dates from the 13th century, and highlights inside the church include not only several magnificent 16th-century Flemish and Florentine tapestries but also the tomb of Bergamo's most famous son, the operatic composer Gaetano Donizetti (1797–1848). Donizetti wrote over 20 operas in his lifetime, and the most famous are probably *Lucia di Lammermoor* and *Don Pasquale*. Considered the king of Italian opera for many years, he was eventually eclipsed by Verdi. Lovers of architecture come to this church from all over the world to admire the ★★★ **Colleoni Chapel**, a Renaissance masterpiece built between 1470 and 1476 by Giovanni Antonio Amadeo, with ceiling frescoes by Tiepolo. Colleoni was a notorious *condottiere* (mercenary) who fought on several different sides during his successful military career, earning enough in the process to have himself suitably immortalised (his equestrian statue can be admired in front of the Scuola San Marco in Venice). Don't leave the Piazza del Duomo without first admiring the polygonal **baptistery**, built in 1340; it used to stand inside Santa Maria Maggiore.

Santa Maria Maggiore

Colleoni Chapel

Donizetti remembered

Stroll westwards now as far as the Piazza Cittadella, where you will find the 13th-century **Citadel** ❸ which today houses a museum of geology and natural history, with several fascinating exhibits. The Torre dei Adalberto in this square was built in the 13th century, and is also known as the 'Tower of Hunger'. Just behind the Citadel, on the other side of the city gate known as the Porta Sant' Alessandro, is the **Donizetti Birthplace Museum** ❹ at No 14, Borgo Canale.

Walk back across the upper town to the Piazza Vecchia, and from there continue eastwards as far as Bergamo's cultural highlight *par excellence*, the ★★ **Accademia Carrara** ❺. This art gallery, founded in the 18th century by Count Giacomo Carrara to house his collection of paintings, contains several superb works by artists such as Titian, Raphael, Botticelli, Velasquez and Mategna – to name but a few. Allow plenty of time for any visit here!

Bergamo's 'lower town' also has several attractions including the church of **San Bartolomeo**, with its large ★ altarpiece by the Late Renaissance artist Lorenzo Lotto (1480–1556). Lotto was famous for his perceptive portraits and mystical paintings of religious subjects. He lived in Bergamo from 1513 onwards, and it was here that his style matured.

Route 7

Lake Iseo *See map, p52–3*

Lake Iseo, situated between Bergamo and Brescia, lies 186m (610ft) above sea level, is 25km (15 miles) long, has a maximum width of 5km (3 miles), a maximum depth of 250m (820ft), and a surface area of 62sq km (24sq miles). Named *Sebinus Lacus* by the Romans, it is the seventh-largest lake in Italy.

This route goes around the lake in a clockwise direction, starting at the small town of **Sarnico**, which already provides a foretaste of the natural scenery in store. The mountains along the western shore descend steeply towards the lake, while the area of reeds across to the east is framed by rolling meadows full of flowers. The uniformity of the landscape is interrupted by the odd colourful campsite, and small sailing boats can often be seen on the dark-green water.

Sarnico

Olive groves, vineyards and avenues of cypress trees line the road, which goes through a series of illuminated tunnels. The steep shore between Tavernola and Riva di Solto is unspoilt. Venice quarried the black marble for San Marco here, and for many years this region was only accessible by boat; the road here was only completed in 1910.

Soon the main town on Lake Iseo comes into view: **Lovere**. This cheerful community has few old buildings, but to make up for that there is an astonishingly good collection of paintings and porcelain at the **Museo Tadini** (May to October daily 3–6pm, Sunday and public holidays 10am–noon). Don't miss the coffee and cake here either – it's absolutely delicious and also far cheaper than in many other places.

Local souvenirs

Life on the water

Ferry to Monte Isola

The eastern shore starts off promisingly, but romance tends to dissipate after the first few miles. The old road winds pleasantly past several old villas along the shore as far as Pisogne, but then suddenly widens to accommodate heavy goods traffic. Don't rush at this point, otherwise you'll miss the 15th-century Augustinian church of ★ **Santa Maria delle Neve**, which contains some excellent fresco work by the Renaissance artist Romanino.

The next stop is **Sulzano**, picturesquely situated beside a yachting harbour, and the starting-point for ferry trips (quarter-hourly until midnight) across to the largest island in any Italian lake, ★★ **Monte Isola**. This 'island-mountain', 600m (1,970ft) high and covered with thick chestnut forest and ancient olive groves, is a haven of tranquillity. To ensure that it remains so, only the locals

are allowed to use the car ferry (Sunday excepted). Those reluctant to do the 3-hr walk around the island can travel by shuttle bus between the tiny communities, and there's also a bicycle hire service. The 40-minute ascent from the village of Peschiera Maraglio to the 16th-century pilgrimage church of **Madonna della Ceriola** is well worth it for the superb view of the sparkling lake below and the two offshore islands of San Paolo and Loreto.

A real highlight completes this brief tour of the lake: ★ **Iseo** itself. The entrance to it via the 15th-century Castello Oldofredi is absolutely delightful. The various narrow alleys meet up at the arcaded Piazza Garibaldi, the town's medieval market-place with its tiny 15th-century church of **Santa Maria del Mercato**. The no less atmospheric

Lakeside houses at Iseo

Bathers and blossoms

Piazza del Sagrato boasts the church of Sant'Andrea, founded in the 5th century and rebuilt in the 12th, and to the right of it is the mausoleum of Giacomo Oldofredi, who was one of the feudal lords of this region during medieval times.

One very rewarding car excursion from the Lago d'Iseo is to **Capo di Ponte**, halfway up the Val Camonica to the northeast, famed for its ★★ **prehistoric rock engravings**. Around 158,000 of these have been discovered, and they date from different periods – some even from Neolithic times (8,000 years ago). The engravings, many of which show hunting scenes and religious symbols, can be admired in Capo di Ponte's National Rock Engravings Park *(Parco Nazionale delle Incisioni Rupestri)*, which was declared a World Heritage Site by UNESCO in 1979.

For another fascinating sight, this time natural rather than man-made, drive inland from the eastern shore road at Marone and visit the attractive little village of **Zone**. Just before the village of Cislano you'll see them: Zone's famous ★★ **erosion pillars**. Created by the deposition of glacial debris, these fascinating natural columns vary in form, and their most unusual features are the boulders perched precariously on top, which make the whole scene even more bizarre.

To the south of Lago d'Iseo, the region of **Franciacorta** with its gentle morraine hills is seldom visited by tourists, but its fine wines and hidden artistic treasures make it a fascinating area to explore. From Iseo the most direct link with Lake Garda (*see opposite*) is provided by the road through Gardone Val Trompia, where the famous Beretta guns are manufactured, and on past the cliffs of Nozza and through Vestone to Lago d'Idro (*see page 70*).

En route to Capo di Ponte...

...a town with a prehistoric past

Route 8

★★★ Lake Garda

Lake Garda, the largest inland lake in Italy, 51km (31 miles) long and up to 17km (10 miles) wide, is regarded by many as the most beautiful of the Northern Italian Lakes. It is 65m (213ft) above sea level. Narrow at its northern end, Lake Garda gradually widens further southwards into a basin that is almost circular, with rich vegetation on its southern and western shores: citrus fruits, laurels, cypresses, vines, oleanders, palm trees and olives all grow here. The lake was referred to as the *Lacus Benacus* by Virgil, Horace and Catullus, but its name changed in the 9th century when the city of Garda was elevated to a county by Charlemagne and acquired dominion over the lake. It is also known as *Benaco*.

Restaurant in Riva

Three Italian provinces border the lake: Trento to the north, Brescia to the west and Verona to the east. This has had a beneficial effect in that each province does its best not to be shown up by the others, and Lake Garda consequently has very well-surfaced roads and also a consistently successful environmental policy ever since the catastrophic pollution of the lake in 1992. The water quality is now acceptable, and a new environmental awareness has taken hold of the entire region.

Lake Garda has an interesting geological history: the glacier that formed it broadened out as it reached the Plain of Lombardy and left a thick layer of moraine. The lake then formed behind this – which explains why the southern part of Lake Garda is relatively shallow in comparison to the deeply gouged northern section (340m/1,110ft). The lake is fed at its northern end by the River Sarca, and at the southern end the River Mincio flows out towards the Po. The entire basin contains 50 million cubic metres of water. There are five islands in Lake Garda, all privately owned: the Isola di Garda (the largest one) in the west measures 9 hectares (22 acres), the Isola San Biagio in the southwest measures only 1 hectare (2½ acres) and the other three – Trimelone, Sogno and dell'Olivo – are so tiny that they don't really merit attention!

Carefree days by the lake

Tourism has had an enormous effect over the past few decades. Lake Garda caters to over 5 million visitors each year, and it's no wonder that the flatter eastern shore is filled with hotels and campsites. The more elegant communities in the north and west are also continuing to expand rapidly and only strict building regulations have managed to halt the construction of faceless apartment blocks and cheap hotels alongside medieval cathedrals. Germans make up the largest contingent of foreign visitors here (62 percent), and when they are joined by the

ROUTE 8
0
10 km
Trentino
Lombardia
Veneto
Parco
dell´ Alto Garda
Bresciano
Lago di Garda
Lago d' Idro
Lago di Ledro
Lago di Valvestino
Val d´Ampola
Val di Ledro
Val d. Caffaro
Valle Toscolano
MONTE BALDO
Madonna di Campiglio
Cologna
Arco
Casc. d. Varone
Riva
M. Brione 376
Nago
Torbole
Pieve di Ledro
Mezzolago
Molina di Ledro
Pre
Biacesa
P.so d´Ampola
Dosso d. Croce 1869
Storo
Darzo
Lodrone
Bagolino
P.te Caffaro
Monte Tremalzo 1974
Limone sul Garda
Vesio
Tremosine
Campione del Garda
Mad. d. Monte Castello
Tignale
Gardola
Isola Trimelone
Malcesine
Cassone
Assenza
Monte Maggiore 2200
S. Antonio
Anfo
Armo
Idro
Lemprato
Capovalle
Lago d' Iseo
Muslone
Liano
Gargnano
Castelletto di Brenzone
Brenzone
Monte Spino 1486
1582 Monte Pizzocolo
Gaino
Vobarno
Toscolano-Maderno
Madonna della Corona
Trento
Gardone Riviera
Salò
S. Zeno di Montagna
Monte Belpo 884
Torri d. Benaco
Albisano
Caprino
Isola di Garda
M. Luppia 418
Costermano
S. Felice del Benaco
S. Vigilio
Garda
Eremo
Pieve Vecchia
Rocca di Manerba
Montinelle
Polpenazze del Garda
Castrezzone
Manerba del Garda
Bardolino
Affi
Cisano
Padenghe sul Garda
Moniga del Garda
Lazise
S. Pietro in Cariano
Adige
Sirmione
Maguzzano
Desenzano del Garda
Lonato
Rivoltella
Peschiera d. Garda
Palazzola
Castelnuovo del Garda
Verona
Brescia
Castiglione d. Stiviere
Pozzolengo
Mincio
Mantova
8a
8c
8d

Italians in the summer not one room is available – even the dog kennels are booked out. It's easy to guess the locals' main source of income. Fortunately, however, the region around the lake has retained its rural character and structure, and just a few miles inland from the holiday resorts there are vineyards, wheat fields and orchards.

8a – The Eastern Shore

Riva – Malcesine – Torri del Benaco – Garda – Sirmione (75km/47miles)

The scenic stretch of road known as the Gardesana Orientale was completed in 1926, but today has sadly become one of the most-travelled routes in the region; mile-long queues are an everyday occurrence in peak season, but generous by-passes are gradually being built to cope with it all. The route is varied from the landscape point of view, leading from Alpine mountains across rolling hills to the broad southern plain, and from the surfing paradises of Riva and Torbole past the mighty Monte Baldo massif and the gentle Bardolino wine region to reach the elegant thermal resort of Sirmione at the end of its narrow peninsula. Much of this route can also be covered by bus, and a day isn't really enough to fully appreciate all the contrasts. It's best to cover the eastern shore in stages, not forgetting the delights of 'real Italy' further inland.

The medieval side of Riva

Tradition and elegance are the two most striking characteristics of ★★ **Riva** (pop. 13,000), situated at the northern end of Lake Garda, where the reflections of the steep foothills of the Alps shimmer in the turquoise water. Riva has long been a favourite of writers and poets. Goethe called it a 'miracle of nature', and was followed here by Stendhal, Kafka, Thomas Mann and DH Lawrence. The town has several interesting sights to offer, and the best place to begin any stroll is the ★ **Piazza Tre Novembre**, facing out towards the lake and the harbour, and dominated by the steep walls of the Monte Rochetta (1,540m/ 4,320ft). The other side of the square is taken up by buildings in the Venetian-Lombard style with pleasantly cool arcades (14th-century) and the 34-m (111-ft) high **Torre Apponale**; this clock tower was formerly part of the town's fortifications. The 15th-century **Town Hall** (Palazzo Municipale) is connected by the Porta Bruciata to the 14th-century Palazzo Pretorio, and the coats of arms of the bishops of Trento and Venice can be seen on their facades.

Its turquoise waters

Torre Apponale

From this square the Via Andrea Maffei leads to the Piazza Garibaldi and then to the Piazza Battisti, with the entrance to the ★ **Rocca**, a moated Scaligeri castle complete with drawbridge. It was built in 1124 and has survived several alterations by the Viscontis, the Scaligeri and the Venetians. Today it houses the municipal library, a concert hall and also the **municipal museum** (Tuesday to Saturday 9am–noon and 2–5.30pm, Sunday and public holidays 10am–noon and 2.30–5.30pm), which includes a collection of fascinating prehistoric finds from the pile dwellings at Lake Ledro (*see page* 71).

Another worthwhile sight in Riva is the ★ **Chiesa dell'Inviolata**, a mighty 18th-century baroque building reached via the battlemented San Michele city gate at the end of the Viale Roma. Relatively unadorned on the outside, this octagonal church has an incredibly ornate baroque interior that is well worth a visit.

Varone Falls and approach

There are several good excursions from Riva, including one to **Arco**, a climbers' paradise. Climbers all descend – or rather ascend – here at the beginning of September each year for the world climbing championships. Arco (pop. 11,000) is 5km (3 miles) north of Lake Garda and is dominated by a 126-m (413-ft) high crag with the ruins of a medieval fortress on top – the panoramic view is magnificent. Or why not visit the ★ **Varone Falls**, only 4km (2 miles) outside Riva? The 'Cascata del Varone' has been eroding 4mm of rock annually for the past 20,000 years, and the result is a very wild and romantic gorge. The waterfall can be admired from two grottoes, and warm, waterproof clothing is recommended. Another good excursion with a magnificent view is to the top of Riva's local mountain, the **Monte Brione** (376m/1,230ft), a good place for hikers and mountain-bikers.

Congregating in Torbole

Further down the lake, **Torbole** is the windsurfing capital of the region, and attracts fans of the sport from all over the world. For non-surfers it isn't the best of places, and can be rather noisy; wind and weather are of course the main subject of conversation here. The 18th-century parish church of Sant'Andrea contains a noteworthy *Martyrdom of St Matthew* by Giambettino Cignaroli above its altar. A short detour from Torbole leads up via the little village of Nago to the so-called ★ **Marmitte dei Giganti**, or 'Giants' Pots' – smooth holes in the rock created during the last Ice Age by swirling pebbles and meltwater.

Malcesine's ancient charm

Now the so-called Riviera degli Olivi begins – the name refers to the stretch of lakeshore where high alpine scenery gently gives way to its Mediterranean equivalent, and the town of ★★ **Malcesine** (pop. 3,500) comes into view. This former fishing village now lives almost exclusively from tourism, but unlike many other communities Malcesine has managed to preserve much of its ancient charm. The Scaligeri, who ruled this town once like the Viscontis

Streets around the castle

before them and the Venetians after them, left a magnificent monument behind: the ★★ **Scaligeri Castle**. Built in the 14th century, this fortress almost cost Goethe his life. Delighted and fascinated by the sight of its mighty battlements, the famous German writer took out his sketch pad – and was immediately placed under arrest on suspicion of being an Austrian spy. Luckily one of the locals recognised his name, and he was released again.

Today the panorama from the top of the 33-m (108-ft) high keep can be enjoyed with impunity. It takes only a few minutes to reach the castle along the picturesque alleys of Malcesine, and the place is still remarkably intact, with an upper and a lower section and also three inner courtyards. The former powder room contains a small Goethe exhibition – in memory of the fact that his *Italian Journey* very nearly came to an end here. Several of his sketches can also be admired. The castle also contains the **Museo del Garda e del Baldo** (daily 9.30am–7pm, November to March weekends only 10am–4pm), containing an exhibition documenting local wildlife.

Down by the harbour

The **Palazzo dei Capitani del Lago** down by the harbour, with its delightful palm garden, was once the seat of the Venetian governors; today it is the town hall. The entrance hall contains a fresco dated 1672 showing the castle of Malcesine crowned by the Lion of St Mark. The coat of arms of the governors and a very valuable wooden ceiling can both be admired in the council chamber on the first floor. The highlight of the 18th-century parish church of **SS Benigno e Caro** is a 16th-century *Pietà* by the Veronese artist Girolamo dai Libri.

Excursions from Malcesine include the exciting cable ropeway trip up **Monte Baldo** (daily every 30 minutes 8am–7pm, October to April 9am–5pm, journey time 10 minutes). The panorama from 1,720m (5,642ft) is quite breathtaking, the restaurants are good, and there's also a botanical garden 1,200m (3,936ft) up the mountain with around 600 different kinds of alpine flower.

The Gardesana continues southwards, lined with hotels, past several small villages like **Cassone** and **Assenza**, as far as **Casteletto**, which is not on the lake but on the other side of the road, on the mountainside. It is a jumble of dark, medieval streets grouped around the Piazza dell'Olivo, with its picturesque houses. South of Casteletto, visit the small 12th-century Romanesque church of **San Zeno**, which is something of an architectural rarity with its two aisles and three apses. It was built above Roman foundations, and the 15th-century frescoes depict biblical scenes.

Calm waters at Cassone

Torri del Benaco: the castle

The harbour town of ★ **Torri del Benaco** (pop. 2,500) is once again dominated by a 14th-century Scaligeri castle, built above the foundations of the Roman fort. The attractively restored castle contains a **museum** (April to May Tuesday to Sunday 9.30am–12.30pm and 2.30–5.30pm; June to September 9.30am–1pm and 4.30–7pm) documenting everything from olive cultivation to prehistoric rock drawings. Just south of the castle is a very old *limonaia*, or lemon garden, which is still in use today. Other nearby sights include the baroque church of SS Pietro e Paolo, with its magnificent organ (1744), and the church of Santissima Trinita (at the upper end of the former Palazzo Gardesana) which contains several very colourful frescoes dating from around 1400.

One very good excursion from Torri del Benaco starts at its suburb of Albisano, and ends up very soon afterwards at one of the most beautiful views of Lake Garda. This place was once referred to as the *Balcone del Garda* by the poet Gabriele d'Annunzio. Just 4km (2 miles) further on is the health resort of **San Zeno di Montagna**, with several cheap hotels – a good tip for everyone eager to flee the bustle of the shoreline. It's also the perfect base for hiking trips up Monte Baldo.

San Zeno di Montagna

Several rock drawings dating from the Bronze Age were discovered in 1964 on ★★ **Monte Luppia** (418m/1,370ft), and over 250 rocks with more than 3,000 drawings have since been found. The rocks depicting swords and armed men are known as *Pietre delle Griselle*, and the ones with horsemen *Pietre dei Cavalieri*. The Monte Luppia Rock Drawings can be reached via the road to Albisano.

Punta San Vigilio delights

Just north of the Bay of Garda, the small promontory that is actually an extension of the Monte Baldo is one of the most delightful parts of Lake Garda: the ★★ **Punta San Vigilio**. The 16th-century Renaissance patrician Agostino di Brenzone had an elegant villa built here in the middle of a magnificent park; unfortunately it is still privately owned today and closed to public access. The house can still be viewed from the avenue of cypresses in the park, however; it's a Renaissance dream come true. The chapel of San Vigilio can only be visited on 25 April each year.

Pizza express

Continue southwards to the little town of ★ **Garda** (pop. 3,500), much appreciated for its medieval streets, trendy boutiques and elegant lake promenade. The exorbitantly high prices in the restaurants and clothes shops don't seem to put people off at all – it must be said straight away that Garda is not the cheapest place in the world. The Rocca di Garda, a 294-m (964-ft) high rocky plateau, stands above the town like some oversized tower. Theodoric, king of the Ostrogoths, had a fortress built on top of it in the 5th century, but a few foundation walls are all that remains of it today. The tower played an important role in Italian history: it was here that Adelheid, the widow of the king Lothar murdered by the Lombard king Berengar II, was held captive before she managed to flee across the lake in 951 and marry King Otto the Great – who duly chased the Lombards off.

Garda is full of noble villas and palazzi, most of which are privately owned. The finest one in town is the **Palazzo dei Capitani** with its Gothic pointed-arch windows, in the Piazza Catullo on the lake promenade. The parish church of **Santa Maria** in the Piazzale Roma outside the old town has a fine 15th-century cloister.

A good excursion destination from Garda is **Eremo Monastery**, founded in the 17th century; it's such a strict place that women still aren't allowed anywhere near it. To get there turn off at an Agip petrol station just outside Bardolino and travel as far as the village of Cortelline. There's a tiny road on the left near a statue of the Virgin which leads straight there.

Bardolino

The 16th-century pilgrimage church of ★ **Madonna della Corona**, is perched precariously 600m (1,970ft) above the Adige Valley. To get there, go via Costermano, which has one of the largest World War II military cemeteries in Italy with over 2,000 graves. The church can be reached easily via Caprino Veronese, Spiazzi and then a short walk of around 1km (½ mile), unless you prefer the shuttle bus. The first chapel was built here in 1530, and heaving the construction materials up the mountainside must have been a very arduous business; in 1988 Pope John Paul II was driven right up to the church door in his luxury limousine. Serious pilgrims take the amazingly steep route via the 450 steps which lead from the Adige Valley up to the church.

Lazing around in Lazise

Next on this route is ★ **Bardolino** (pop. 6,000), at the centre of a wine region famed for its delicious Italian reds that are easily on a par with *Chianti* or *Barolo*, as can be judged at one or more of the numerous tastings along the *Strada del Vino* which makes its well-signposted way past 43 different vineyards. Highlights of the town of Bardolino include the Romanesque church of ★ **San Severo**, with its mighty campanile. The renditions of courtly battles, the Passion and the Apocalypse are amazingly lifelike. Beyond the high altar the crypt has been excavated to reveal an earlier Lombard structure. The chapel of **San Zeno** (Via San Zeno 13–15) is tucked away in a courtyard, but don't miss it: the building dates from the 9th century, and is one of the oldest surviving Carolingian structures in Italy.

Romanesque San Severo

The romantic little town of ★ **Lazise** (pop. 5,500) has some well-preserved walls and a six-towered Scaligeri castle (12th-century, privately owned); under Venetian rule it was the most important trading post on the lake and also the first independent commune. A 14th-century Venetian custom house and the 12th-century Romanesque church of **San Niccolò** both still stand as reminders of Lazise's heyday. For something a bit different, why not take the children to see the full-size replica dinosaurs in the **Garda Safari Park** at Pastrengo?

Guarding the town gate

The former fishing village of **Peschiera del Garda** (pop. 9,000) has also been strategically important since Roman times, and the 2.3-km (1½-mile) long bastion walls around its old centre were first built during Venetian times, and later strengthened by Napoleon and the Austrians. The best way to appreciate their sheer size is to take a boat trip along the moats.

The town of ★★★ **Sirmione** (pop. 4,000) is like something straight out of a fairytale. It lies at the very end of a flat, 4-km (2½-mile) long peninsula which widens at the end to form three rocky crags rising from the brilliant blue of the water. The bright colours of the flowers, and the green of olives, laurels and cypresses combine with the red of the rooftops and the soft light to create a unique Mediterranean atmosphere, all of it set against the incomparable beauty of the high Alps in the distance.

Sirmione's Scaligeri castle

The old centre can either be reached along the peninsula road, with its hotels and supermarkets, or more romantically by boat from Desenzano. The first sight that strikes visitors here is the forbidding-looking ★★ **Scaligeri moated castle**, without a doubt the best-preserved fortress in all Italy. It was built by Mastino I della Scala in 1250, above the foundations of the former Roman harbour. A massive 30-m (98-ft) high keep towers above the castle walls, and there's a stunning ★ panorama from the top that takes in the peninsula and the whole southern half of Lake Garda. The **castle museum** (April to September Monday to Saturday 9am–12.30pm and 2–6pm, Sunday and public holidays 9am–12.30pm, October to March 9am–1pm) contains several finds from antiquity and also a 15th-century Venetian galley.

San Pietro in Mavino

The old town, with its jumble of alleyways and picturesque houses, is reached through just one gate, and the lake can be glimpsed now and then between the buildings. The whole place gets less busy at the thermal baths – an ugly, purpose-built structure – and there are several gardens on the way down to the Grotte di Catullo. High up on the nearby hill is the small Romanesque church of ★ **San Pietro in Mavino**, built by Lombard monks in the 8th century; the frescoes date from the 12th to the 16th centuries, and there is a particularly impressive *Last Judgement* (daily 8am–sunset). At the very end of the peninsula are the remains of an enormous Roman villa (230m/750ft long, 105m/345ft wide), the so-called ★★ **Grotte di Catullo**. Little appreciated in his day because of his somewhat daring amorous verse, Catullus (87–54BC) knew of this complex of buildings, which was probably an imperial guest house or even an imperial palace, complete with its own thermal baths. He was far too poor ever to have lived here, however. A large swimming pool in the vast complex was fed by the Boiola springs on the lake shore via lead piping. The sulphurous springs were rediscovered in the 16th century, but only re-used 300 years later. Since that time, visitors to Sirmione have been able to enjoy the Ancient Roman pleasure of bathing in hot spring water. The small museum (summer daily except Monday 9am–6pm, winter 9am–4pm) provides a good idea of what the Roman complex must have looked like.

Grotte di Catullo

8b: Southern end of the lake – Battle sites

Peschiera del Garda – Custoza – Solferino – San Martino della Battaglia – Sirmione (60km/40miles)

These days there are no sounds of battle to spoil the tranquillity of the plain south of Sirmione, which is one of the best-kept secrets of Lake Garda. There are reminders of the wars of liberation against the Austrians all over the place, in villages such as Custoza and Solferino. The latter battle, fought in 1859, was so bloody that it resulted in the formation of the Red Cross. This round trip can also be done in bad weather, and if so it should be combined with a trip across to Verona to view the sights there.

Custoza and its ossarium

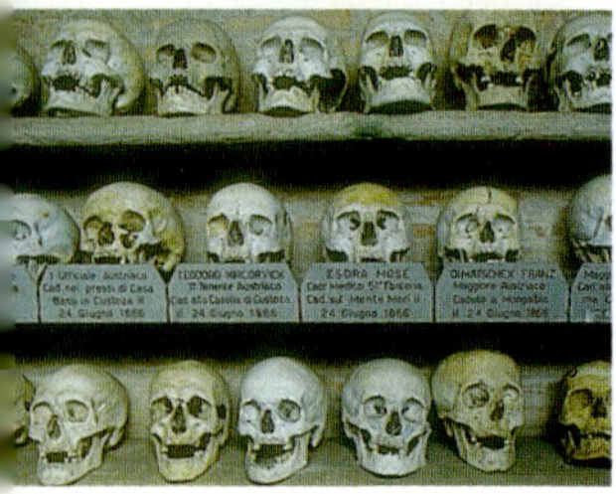

Before following the River Mincio across its green meadows, take a short detour to the tiny **Laghetto di Frassino**, and to one of the most delightful pilgrimage churches in the region, ★ **Madonna del Frassino**, built in the early 16th century. Legend has it that the Virgin Mary appeared in an ash tree *(frassino)* here in May 1510 and saved a wine farmer from a poisonous snake. The side-chapel containing a miracle-working Madonna sculpture is filled with thousands of candles. From the church, the route continues southeastwards at the little village of Salionze.

Surrounded by meadows and vineyards, ★**Custoza** lies on a small rise. Former battle sites such as these are known in Italy as *Zona Sacra*, or 'holy zones'. The monument with its enormous obelisk, commemorating the senseless death of thousands of soldiers, can be seen from far away. It was in July 1848 that Count Radetzky's Austrian troops inflicted a crushing defeat on Italy's freedom-fighters. An *ossarium* (daily except Tuesday 9am–noon, November to February 2–3pm, March and October 2.30–5pm, April to September 3.15–7pm) to house the remains of the fallen was built here three decades later, and today it contains the bones of 3,200 soldiers of both nations.

The next stop on this route is ★★ **Borghetto di Valeggio sul Mincio**, a sleepy village in the shade of Valeggio's Scaligeri castle which was chosen 600 years ago

as the site of a demonstration of power. In 1393 Giangaleazzo Visconti decided to build a gigantic dam to deprive the cities of Mantua and Verona of water. The dimensions are amazing: the ★★ **Ponte Visconteo**, as the dam is called, is 600m (2,000ft) long, 26m (85ft) wide and 10m (32ft) high, and it took just eight months to build. It's worth taking a stroll across the dam, with its gates and towers, to get a close-up impression of this astonishing medieval achievement.

In 1438 not even the Venetians dared attack the Ponte Visconteo to help besieged Brescia fight the Visconti. Instead, Venice was clever and bold enough to transport its warships across the mountains – and then re-float them near Torbole. Imagine the scene: 2,000 oxen pulling 6 galleys, 2 galleons and 26 barques across the Nago Pass to Lake Garda! Those interested in learning more about this amazing feat should visit the exhibition at the castle in Malcesine (*see page 58*).

One good nearby excursion destination is the ★★ **Parco Giardino Sigurtà** (Thursday, Saturday, Sunday and public holidays March to November 9am–sunset), an English-style park in Veneto covering 50 hectares (123 acres). Small lakes, viewing terraces, a hermitage church and yet another ruined Scaligeri castle – they're all here. Everything about the place is sheer paradise in fact, except the admission fee.

Solferino

It was at the bloody battle of ★ **Solferino** in June 1859 (*see page 11*) that Henri Dunant, a merchant from Geneva, decided to found the Red Cross *(Croce Rossa)*. He received the Nobel Peace Prize for his efforts near the end of his life, in 1901, and promptly bequeathed the prize money to his Red Cross organisation. The great humanist did not live to see the horrors of World War I; he died in 1910 in the canton of Appenzell. The **Chiesa San Pietro in Vincoli** contains the remains of around 7,000 soldiers who fell here. By way of contrast, the **Museo Storico** (daily except Monday 8.30am–1pm and 2.30–8.30pm) documents the glorious side of war, with plenty of weapons, uniforms, etc. The ★ **Piazza Castello**, one of the finest squares in the province of Mantua, was formerly occupied by an 11th-century castle. All that remains of the original building today is one watchtower with an oriental-style pointed cupola. The marble Red Cross Memorial, erected here in 1959, can be reached along an avenue of cypresses.

Remnants of battle at San Martino della Battaglia

The last famous battle site in this region is **San Martino della Battaglia**, which shared Solferino's fate in 1859. A 74-m (242-ft) high tower stands in memory of the horrors of war. Inside, wall frescoes document the history of the Italian freedom fighters from 1848 to 1870.

Desenzano del Garda – Salò – Gardone Riviera – Limone – Riva (70km/44 miles) *See map, p56*

From Salò to Riva alone, a total of 70 tunnels had to be blown out of the rock to build the road along Lake Garda's western shore. Car drivers may be rather confused at all the light and shade, but passengers will glimpse a whole series of superb Mediterranean-style vistas. Even in heavy traffic the route can easily be covered in an hour, not including detours. Visiting only a few of the sights can easily take up a day, however.

Desenzano del Garda harbour

Restoring Roman mosaics

Desenzano drifters

The town of ★ **Desenzano del Garda** (pop. 20,000) at the southwestern end of Lake Garda is the largest and also the liveliest community on the lake. A harbour since Roman times, the town is still a busy trading centre. Its enormous market is held every Tuesday on the Cesare Battisti lake promenade; the selection of wares is vast, and the prices are very reasonable. A few steps away from the main square, at the end of the Via Scavi Romano, are the ruins of a ★ **Villa Romana** (April to September daily except Monday 9am–6.30pm, October to March 9am–sunset) dating from the 3rd century AD. The 240sq m (2,600sq ft) of mosaic floor reveal the sheer magnificence of Roman lifestyles during Late Antiquity. It's also worth visiting the 16th-century parish church of **Santa Maria Maddalena** (daily 7am–noon and 3.30–7pm) on the Piazza del Duomo; it contains an impressive early work by Tiepolo, *The Last Supper*, in a side chapel.

Those acquainted with military history will enjoy an excursion from Desenzano to **Lonato** (pop. 10,900), a typical Lombard town 10km (6 miles) to the west. It was here in 1796 that Napoleon inflicted a crushing defeat on the Austrians. There is a superb panoramic view across the

Plain of Lombardy from the ruined fortress. On the way up there you'll pass the ★ **Casa del Podestà** (Monday to Friday 9am–noon and 2–4pm), which was richly furnished during the 19th century with furniture, paintings and over 30,000 books by the politician, historian and art collector Ugo da Como.

Just 5km (3 miles) north of Lonato is the ★ **Abbazia di Maguzzano**, a formerly Benedictine abbey built in the 9th century, destroyed in 922 by the Huns and then plundered yet again by the Visconti in the 14th century. It received its present appearance in the 15th century, and the church and cloister are quite magnificent. Dissolved by Napoleon in 1797, the abbey fell into decay before being rescued in 1904, when it was purchased by the Cistercian Order. Despite its proximity to busy Lonato, the abbey is marvellously peaceful.

North of Desenzano is the rolling landscape known as the Valtenesi, a fertile region famous for its pale red *Chiaretto* wines. Ruined fortresses on the hilltops testify to its violent past, however. **Moniga del Garda**, hidden behind its battlemented walls dating from the years of fighting between the Visconti and the Scaligeri, is one of the most attractive Valtenesi communities. **Manerba del Garda** is a tourist centre, and there's a good view to be had from the ruined **Rocca di Manerba** (280m/918ft) near Montinelle. Don't miss the 15th-century pilgrimage church of ★ **Santa Maria del Carmine**, situated 13km (7 miles) north of Pieve Vecchia in the middle of a vineyard region; it contains a fine *Annunciation* by a local 15th-century artist as well as a delightful wooden Madonna.

Continue now to the delightful town of ★★ **Salò** (pop. 9,800). Most of its architectural treasures survived the earthquake of 1901 unscathed, and a stroll here is definitely worthwhile. Start off at the 15th-century cathedral of **Santa Maria Annunziata** (daily 8am–noon and 3–6pm), the most important Late Gothic structure in the region. Note the 11-m (36-ft) high Gothic-Venetian dome, which measures 44m (144ft) across. Highlights inside the cathedral include a Late Gothic crucifix dating from 1449, and an interesting *St Antony of Padua* by the Renaissance painter Romanino (1486–1560), in which the artist breaks with convention by portraying his patron most unflatteringly as a fat, unpleasant-looking man at St Antony's feet; even the angels seem to be averting their gazes.

Not far from the cathedral, through a magnificent arcade built by the Venetian architect Sansovino, are the 14th-century Palazzo della Podestà (town hall) and the 16th-century Palazzo della Magnifica Patria, which today houses the **Museo Civico Archeologico** (summer daily except Monday 10am–noon and 5–7pm, October to March weekends only).

Manerba from the Rocca

Salo: Santa Maria Annunziata

Salò is also famous – or rather infamous – historically as the place where Mussolini's Nazi-supported puppet government continued to rule a reluctant Italy from 1943 onwards; its sphere of influence dwindled steadily as the German troops were forced back. When the German front in northern Italy finally crumbled, Mussolini was forced to flee to Switzerland with his mistress Clara Petacci. They were caught by partisans in Dongo, on Lake Como, and summarily executed in Mezzegra (*see page 41*).

The town of ★ **Gardone Riviera** (pop. 2,500) no longer resembles the fishing village it once was, mainly because of the German architect Ludwig Wimmer who built the Grand Hotel Gardone Riviera here in 1880. The upper part of town contains the **Vittoriale** (May to August 9am–12.30pm and 2–6pm, June to September 9am–12.30 and 2–6.30pm; admission exorbitantly expensive), a bombastic monument commissioned just before the war by Fascist Italy's most celebrated poet, Gabriele d'Annunzio. The rooms are an amazing mixture of priceless antiques and glorified kitsch; in short, the Vittoriale is a gloomy monument to its owner's megalomania. The complex includes a theatre, a columned hall with the owner's tomb, a domed structure for the private plane d'Annunzio used to distribute leaflets above Vienna in 1918, a museum full of memorabilia, and also a ship – or rather the bow section of one. It is part of the battleship *Puglia*, filled with cement and uncannily realistic.

Botanical delights at Gardone

By way of a change, only a few steps away from the Vittoriale is the wonderfully peaceful ★ **Giardino Botanico** (March to October 9am–7pm; admission fee). It was laid out in 1910, and its waterfalls, ponds and bridges make it an oasis of tranquillity.

Sant'Andrea

The main attraction of **Toscolano-Maderno** is the 12th-century parish church of ★★ **Sant'Andrea**, on the lake promenade in Maderno. Fragments of an Early Christian temple and also the remains of an earlier Lombard structure can be recognised from the facade, apse and westwork. The entrance portal has some very fine sculpture work. Toscolano, the other half of this twin-town, grew rich during medieval times by making metal components for Venetian galleys, and then even richer from its paper and printing industry which started here in the 15th century and is still flourishing today.

The picturesque town of ★ **Gargnano** (pop. 3,300) has so far been left relatively unscathed by tourism. From 1943 to 1945 the neoclassical Palazzo Feltrinelli housed the ministries of the fascist 'Republic of Salò'; today it is where Milan University holds its language courses during the summer. Fifty years ago Mussolini lived in the **Villa Feltrinelli**, just a short walk away; today it's closed to public access. Another highlight of Gargnano is the so-called 'stone lemon garden' (late July to late August daily 10am–1pm and 3–8pm, otherwise 9am–6pm) in the late 13th-century Romanesque-Gothic cloister of San Francesco, where citrus fruit can be seen adorning the capitals in place of the usual demons and gargoyles.

Villa Feltrinelli

For adventurous motorists, there's a nice excursion from Gargnano to the 13th-century (later baroqueified) pilgrimage church of ★★ **Madonna di Monte Castello**. Situated 700m (2,290ft) above sea level, it lies at the end of a road full of bends, and there's a brief gradient of 26 percent just before you arrive. The church was built above the ruins of a Scaligeri fortress, and the ★★ view is absolutely incredible. From here, continue on to ★ **Tremosine**, the collective name for several villages in the wild and romantic Campione valley. Many coins and also the 'Stone of Voltino', with Latin and Etruscan inscriptions (now in the Roman Museum in Brescia), were found here, testifying to settlement of this region as far back as antiquity. In those days it was used as a place of refuge, and today the area is still off the beaten track; its hairpin bends continue to deter tourist buses.

Madonna di Monte Castello

A warning at this point to all motorists without a head for heights: the roads often pass amazingly steep drops and require not only good nerves but also good driving abilities. In bad weather they should be avoided completely because of the danger of falling rocks. Just remember that the Italian word for 'gorge' is *orrido*...

You need a good head for heights

Of all the small villages with incredibly good views around here, **Pieve** deserves special mention. Those prone to vertigo should avoid dining in Pieve's 'Miralago' restaurant, despite the excellent food the restaurant terrace juts out above a vertical drop of 350m (1,148ft).

Hooting before each hairpin on the way back from Pieve to the road round the lake isn't just recommended – it's obligatory. The narrow road, lined with waterfalls and ravines, is just wide enough for one car.

Back down at the lake, the town of **Limone sul Garda** is not what it once was. Formerly the lemon garden of Lake Garda, it has now sold its soul completely to tourism, and the *limonaie* (greenhouses for lemon-growing) that once cheered the place up are very thin on the ground these days. The old parish church of **San Benedetto** (17th-century) in the centre is worth a visit for Andrea Celesti's *Three Magi* on the right of the altar. By the way, don't leave Limone sul Garda without sampling its delicious carp dishes, flavoured – of course – with lemon.

Limone sul Garda

Gargnano – Lago di Valvestino – Lago d'Idro – Lago di Ledro (80km/50 miles) *See map, p56*

If the noisy shores of Lake Garda prove too much of a strain on the nerves, what better way to wind down than to take a trip to some of Lombardy's smaller lakes? Generally speaking, mass tourism has passed them by. This route leads from Gargnano on Lake Garda to the Lago di Valvestino (actually a reservoir) near Gargnano, on to the Lago d'Idro which only has communities along its western bank, up to the tiny Lago di Ledro with its prehistoric pile dwellings and then back to Lake Garda. Allow three hours for the trip.

Fishing on Idro

Flowers for sale

From Gargnano, travel the short distance to **Lake Valvestino**, a reservoir set between the Val Toscolano and the valley of the Valvestino. The shimmering green, fjord-like waters of the lake contrast most impressively with the dam, and the whole scene is framed against magnificent mountain scenery. There are great views to be had from the top of Monte Caplone, reached from Magasa.

The next lake on the route is the ★ **Lago d'Idro**, known to the Romans as the *Lacus Eridius*. The steep mountain cliffs that surround the Lago d'Idro seem to rise straight out of the water in places, and some sections of shore are impassable. Situated 318m (1,043ft) above sea level, the lake is roughly 10km (6 miles) long, up to 2km (1 mile) wide, and 122m (400ft) deep. The Lago d'Idro is the highest of all the Italian lakes, but its water temperature is astonishingly similar to that of Lake Garda, reaching around 25°C (77°F) during the summer. It is particularly renowned for its trout.

Lake Idro is particularly popular with campers, and there are several sites dotted around the main resort village of **Idro**; one of the best is the Campeggio Venus. The nearby village of **Anfo** is rather more attractive than Idro itself, and is very popular with sailing enthusiasts. Just outside the village, up on the **Rocca d'Anfo**, is a castle originally built by the Venetians during the 15th century; since then it has undergone quite a lot of alteration. In 1866 Garibaldi used it as his headquarters, and during World War I it was used for military purposes again in the fight against the Austrians. The small chapel of **Sant'Antonio** nearby contains 13th- and 14th-century frescoes, but is usually closed. Ponte Caffaro, 2km (1 mile) before the northern tip of the lake, is where the Counts of Lodron did battle first with the Milanese and then the Venetians, and Italy's former border with the then Austrian-ruled Trentino used to be located here until 1918.

There's a good detour 16km (10 miles) westwards at this point to ★★ **Bagolino**, which was very wealthy in medieval times because of the iron ore mined in this valley. The detour there begins with several superb views across the lake, and Bagolino not only has some fine churches but also several magnificent town houses, reflecting the prosperity of its medieval population.

Coffee time

Continue along the western shore of Lake Idro now and at Ca Rossa, turn right on to the road leading to Lake Ledro. This route takes you through the Val d'Ampola, past several waterfalls and high mountain peaks (Monte Cadria, 2,254m/7,395ft) as it winds its way steadily uphill. From Tiarno the road then descends again to ★ **Lake Ledro**.

Lake Ledro is only 3km (2 miles) long, 1km (½ mile) wide and up to 48m (150ft) deep, but is surrounded by some stunning mountain scenery and is also important historically as the site of several lake dwellings. For centuries the fishermen of Lake Ledro were irritated by the wooden stakes that kept getting caught in their nets, but no-one realised what the wood was actually doing there. When the water level was lowered in 1929 during a hydroelectric project the remains of over 15,000 piles were discovered. It turned out that people had lived here in 1700BC in a prehistoric village on the lake, and the piles had supported the entire structure. Pottery and other finds are on display in the ★ **Lake Dwelling Museum** (March to June and September to November daily except Monday 9am–noon and 2–6pm; July to August 9am–noon and 3–7pm; December weekends only 9am–noon and 2–5pm; January and February closed) in the village of **Molina di Ledro**.

From Lake Ledro it's not far to the Cascata del Ponale waterfall and back to Lake Garda.

Lago di Ledro with pile dwelling

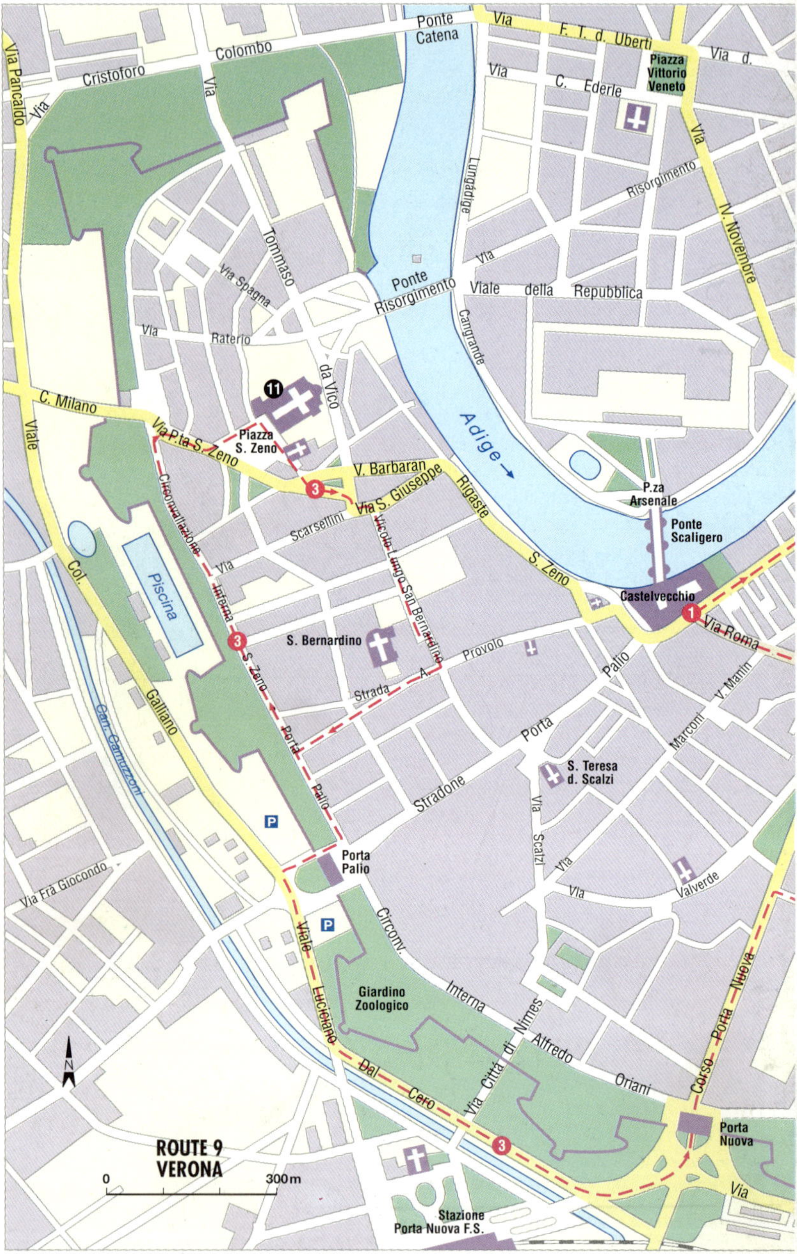
ROUTE 9
VERONA
0
300m
N
Via Pancaldo
Via Cristoforo Colombo
Ponte Catena
Via F. T. d. Uberti
Via d.
Piazza Vittorio Veneto
Via C. Ederle
Via Risorgimento
Via IV. Novembre
Lungadige
Via Tommaso da Vico
Via Spagna
Via Raterio
Ponte Risorgimento
Viale della Repubblica
Cangrande
Adige
C. Milano
Viale Col. Galliano
Via P.ta S. Zeno
Piazza S. Zeno
V. Barbaran
Via S. Giuseppe
Rigaste S. Zeno
P.za Arsenale
Ponte Scaligero
Castelvecchio
Via Roma
Circonvallazione
Via Infera
Scarsellini
Vicolo Lungo San Bernardino
Piscina
S. Bernardino
Strada A. Provolo
Palio
V. Manin
Marconi
S. Zeno - Porta Palio
Stradone Porta Palio
S. Teresa d. Scalzi
Via Scalzi
Via Valverde
Can. Camuzzoni
Porta Palio
Via Frà Giocondo
Viale Luciano Dal Cero
Circonv. Interna
Giardino Zoologico
Via Città di Nimes
Alfredo Oriani
Corso Porta Nuova
Porta Nuova
Via
Stazione Porta Nuova F.S.

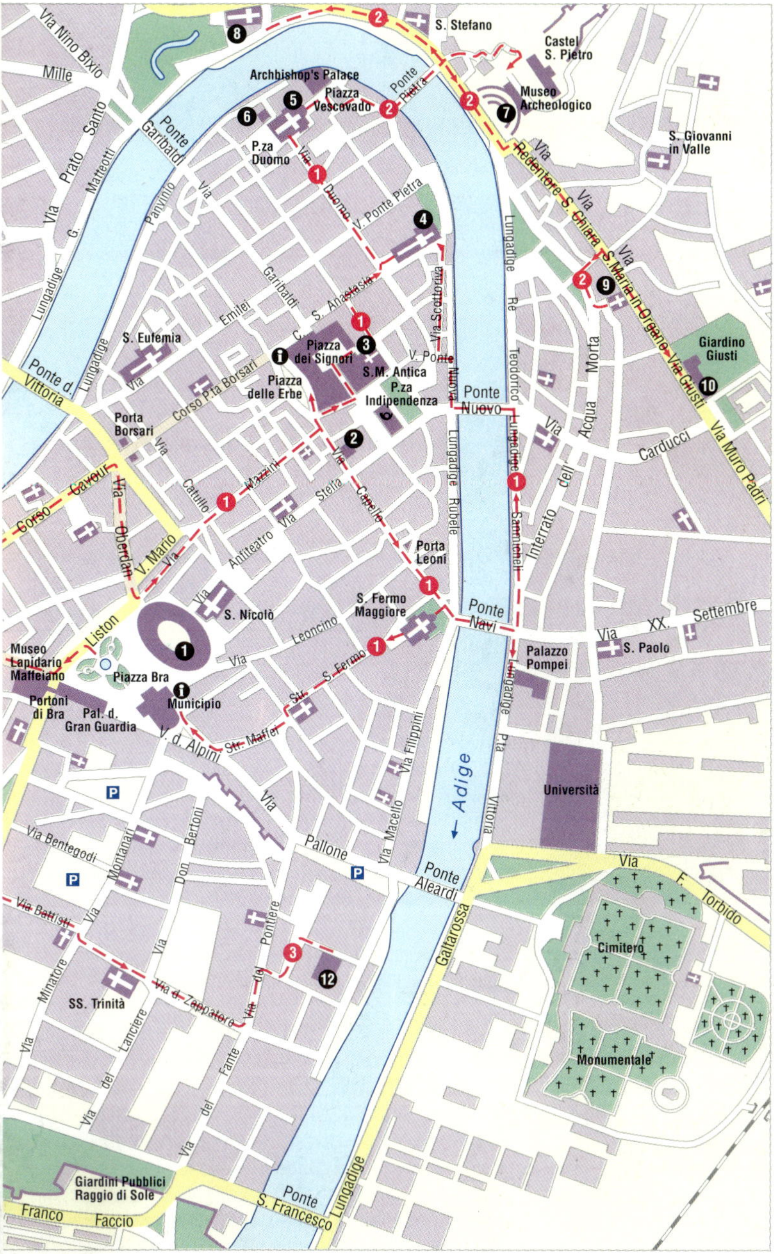
Via Nino Bixio
Mille
S. Stefano
Castel
S. Pietro
Archbishop's Palace
Piazza
Vescovado
Ponte
Pietra
Museo
Archeologico
S. Giovanni
in Valle
Ponte
Garibaldi
P.za
Duomo
Via
Duomo
Via
Prato
Santo
G.
Marteotti
Panvinio
V. Ponte Pietra
Via
Redentore
S. Chiara
Via
S. Maria in Organo
Lungadige
Re
Teodorico
Garibaldi
S. Anastasia
Emilei
S. Eufemia
Piazza
dei Signori
S.M. Antica
P.za
Indipendenza
Via Scottoriva
V. Ponte
Nuova
Ponte
Nuovo
Giardino
Giusti
Via Giusti
Morta
Acqua
dell'
Interrato
Carducci
Via Muro Padri
Ponte d.
Vittoria
Lungadige
Piazza
delle Erbe
Corso P.ta Borsari
Porta
Borsari
Corso
Cavour
Via
Oberdan
Catullo
Mazzini
Via
Stella
Capello
Lungadige
Rubele
Lungadige
Sammicheli
V. Mario
Anfiteatro
Porta
Leoni
S. Nicolò
S. Fermo
Maggiore
Ponte
Navi
Via
XX.
Settembre
S. Paolo
Palazzo
Pompei
Leoncino
Via
S. Fermo
Liston
Museo
Lapidario
Maffeiano
Piazza Bra
Municipio
Portoni
di Bra
Pal. d.
Gran Guardia
V. d. Alpini
Str. Maffei
Str.
Via Filippini
Adige
Lungadige
P.ta
Vittoria
Università
Via
Pallone
Via Macello
Via Bentegodi
Montanari
Don
Bertoni
Ponte
Aleardi
Via
F.
Torbido
Via Battisti
Pontiere
Via
del
Galtarossa
Cimitero
Monumentale
Minatore
SS. Trinità
Via d. Zappatore
Lanciere
Fante
Via
del
Giardini Pubblici
Raggio di Sole
Franco
Faccio
Ponte
S. Francesco
Lungadige

Wet night at the Opera

Route 9

★★ Verona

Juliet's house

Situated on a sharp bend in the River Adige, Verona is an ancient city with Roman remains that are second only to those of Rome itself. It was also a renowned centre of painting in medieval times, but is perhaps most famous of all as the backdrop to Shakespeare's *Romeo and Juliet*.

History

Verona is located at a point of great strategic significance, at the junction of main roads between Italy and Europe. In 89BC it became a Roman colony, and this marked the start of its 'Golden Age', which lasted as long as Roman rule itself: from the 1st century BC to the 5th century AD. During this time *Colonia Augusta* received its municipal charter, became the capital of Cisalpine Gaul and developed into an important trade and administration centre. After the Romans left it was occupied by the Visigoths, then the Byzantines, and then the Lombards. After a Carolingian interlude the Lombards returned once more.

Medieval times were beset by feuds between rival families. In 1262 the della Scalas gained the upper hand and ruled for over a century. It was during this period that the Scaligeri castles were built which have been such a striking feature of the region to this day. Peace returned when Verona voluntarily submitted to Venetian domination in 1405, and it continued until the arrival of the French in 1796. After Napoleon's defeat in 1814, Verona found itself in Austrian hands and the fortifications were strengthened. 1866 brought Italian unification, and although the Austrians still clung on until 1914, their final hopes were dashed by the outbreak of World War I.

City Tour 1 – The Centre

This tour begins at the **Piazza Bra**. It's the longest of the three and also contains the most sights, so half a day would be best. Entrance fees are usually charged for the sights, sometimes L3,000, sometimes up to three times that amount.

Verona's famous ★★ **Arena** ❶ (daily except Monday 8am–6.30pm; during summer festival July and August 8am–1.30pm only), built in 50BC, is the second largest in the world after the Coliseum in Rome. Originally it was 152m (715ft) long, 123m (403ft) wide and could accommodate 30,000 spectators. Today, two thousand years and several earthquakes later, it is still 138m (452ft) long and 109m (357ft) wide, and still has room for 20,000 people.

Even those with very little time to sightsee should definitely not miss ★ **Castelvecchio**, the largest structure dating from Scaligeri times, which today houses the ★ **Museo Civico d'Arte** (daily except Monday 8am–6.30pm), Verona's most famous art museum. It contains works by masters of the Veronese and Venetian schools from the 13th to the 18th century (paintings by Pisanello, Veronese, Titian, Mantegna and Tintoretto), all hung magnificently.

At the end of the Via Mazzini, Verona's most elegant shopping street, is the famous ★ **Casa di Giulietta** ❷ (daily except Monday 8am–6.30pm) with the most famous balcony in the world (Via Capello No 23), where Shakespeare's Juliet is supposed to have lived.

Today's picturesque ★★ **Piazza delle Erbe** used to be the old Roman forum, and the architecture here is wonderfully harmonious. The Gothic Colonna del Mercato is a 14th-century obelisk with the Visconti coat of arms; the Capitello, a late 15th-century marble baldachin in the centre of the square, was used as an official meeting-place and also as a pillory in its time. The market fountains also merit attention, as do the various official and very elegant palazzi all round the square.

A high arch, the Arco della Costa, marks the entrance to the ★ **Piazza dei Signori**. The Venetian governor used to reside in the Renaissance Palazzo del Tribunale (1530). Today the Palazzo del Governo is the seat of the provincial government. Dante lived here in 1303, and the café named after him, next door to the magnificent Loggia del Consiglio, is a good place to soak up the impressive atmosphere. The next small square, the Piazzaletto delle Arche, contains the Gothic graves of the Scaligeri, the ★ **Arche degli Scaligeri** ❸, concealed behind wrought-iron grilles. There are even some set into the facade of the 12th-century Romanesque church of Santa Maria Antica. By the way, **Romeo's house** (12th-century) is just a stone's throw away, at Nos 2–4, Via Arche Scaligeri.

Piazza Bra facade

Arena arches

Museum exhibit

Arche degli Scaligeri

Basilica Sant' Anastasia, detail

The ★ **Basilica Sant'Anastasia** ❹ was completed in the 15th century at the end of the arcaded Via Sottoriva by the Dominican Order. Its sacristy contains Pisanello's celebrated *St George Fresco* (15th-century). Not far away is the ★ **Cathedral of Santa Maria Matricolare** ❺, originally a Romanesque structure built above a 5th-century Early Christian church. Don't miss the superbly colourful ★ *Assumption of the Virgin* by Titian in the first side-chapel to the left.

Next door to the cathedral is the ★★ **Biblioteca Capitulare** ❻ (daily except Thursday and Sunday 9.30am–12.30pm, Tuesday and Wednesday also 4–6pm, closed in July), thought to be the oldest surviving library in the world, with manuscripts dating from the 4th and 5th centuries and wonderful miniatures.

City Tour 2 – Along the Adige

Ponte Pietra

This tour starts on the other side of the **Ponte Pietra** and leads to the best viewpoints in the city. Walking the route takes at least 3 hours, doing it by car takes around 1 hour (parking spaces are available).

On the other side of the bridge on the left is Santo Stefano, founded in the 11th century and one of the oldest churches in Verona, and almost straight ahead are the ruins of the **Teatro Romano** ❼. Built in AD10, the Roman theatre was used as a quarry in medieval times, then forgotten about and only re-excavated in the 19th century. Shakespeare plays are often performed in the ruins here during the summer.

The **archaeological museum** (daily except Monday, summer 8am–6.30pm, winter 8am–2pm) up in the monastery of San Girolamo is worth visiting not only for the finds but also for the magnificent view across the city.

The 15th-century church of ★★ **San Giorgio Maggiore** ❽, with its cupola by Sanmicheli, has been described as the finest Renaissance building in Verona. Highlights inside include a *Baptism of Christ* by Tintoretto and a *Martyrdom of St George* altar painting by Veronese. During his Italian Journey, Goethe noted that San Giorgio was 'a gallery full of good paintings'.

Palazzo Giusti

The next two stops on the tour are further up the Adige: firstly the church of ★ **Santa Maria in Organo** ❾, formerly Benedictine, which gained its earliest written mention in 866, and received its Renaissance splendour from Sanmicheli at the end of the 15th century; and secondly the ★ **Palazzo Giusti** ❿ (summer daily 9am–8pm, winter 9am–sunset), a beautifully situated 16th-century palazzo, high up above the city in terraced grounds, with a stunning panoramic view.

San Zeno Maggiore: bronze door

City Tour 3 – Further Sights

The starting-point for this tour is the Porta Palio, a city gate dating from the 16th century. Drive round the Circonvallazione to the Piazza San Zeno and the basilica of ★★★ **San Zeno Maggiore** ⓫. Only superlatives can be used to describe this, the most magnificent Romanesque church in Northern Italy. After a previous building on the site was destroyed in the 9th century, the new basilica was completed in 1138 and consecrated to Verona's first bishop and patron St Zeno. The reliquary of this Black African saint lies under a marble sculpture dating from 1300 to the left of the apse in the crypt. Of the incredible number of 12th to 14th-century frescoes inside the basilica, the ★ *Madonna and Saints* triptych by Andrea Mantegna (15th-century) deserves special mention; the music-making angels at the Virgin Mary's feet have marvellously touching expressions!

The facade of the basilica is quite magnificent. The ★★ bronze door with its 48 reliefs and the ★★ stone reliefs by Master Nicolò (12th-century) on either side of the portal are utterly fascinating. Inside, the left-hand side-aisle leads off to a very fine ★ cloister.

Juliet's empty tomb

The last sight on this route is the ★ **Tomba di Giulietta** ⓬. Legend has it that Romeo and Juliet were secretly married in the former Franciscan monastery on the Via del Pontiere. In the middle of an atmospheric courtyard stands an old fountain into which visitors can throw coins; in the crypt an empty (!) stone sarcophagus is labelled the 'Tomb of Juliet', and regularly receives written petitions from lovers from all over the world. The small museum here is worth a visit though: the **Museo degli Alfreschi** (daily except Monday 7.30am–6.45pm) has an extensive collection of frescoes and also altar paintings and Roman amphorae.

BIRRA FORST
VR 958163
VR-931249

Art History

Early Architecture

Architecture in the Northern Italian Lakes region began with early lake dwellings such as those discovered in Lake Ledro, not far from Lake Garda. It was around the same time that the rock drawings appeared on Monte Luppia and at Capo di Ponte in the Val Camonica north of Lake Iseo. Later the Romans came and left several magnificent monuments behind; Verona has the second-largest amount of Roman ruins after Rome itself. The ruined villa at Desenzano, the thermal baths in Sirmione and the Arena in Verona all bring antiquity back to life.

The most common material in the lakes region was used to create its most enduring architectural masterpieces: stone. One good early example of just how gifted the local masons were after the collapse of the Roman Empire is the 5th-century baptistery in Riva San Vitale, the oldest sacred building on Swiss soil.

Romanesque

In the area around Lakes Maggiore and Como during the 12th and 13th centuries, it was the Lombard craftsmen known collectively as the *Maestri Comacini* who determined the local style. These expert stone masons, who hailed from Como and are known to have been working at least as long ago as the 7th century, also began to influence styles throughout Europe, establishing a legacy that was to continue right up to the Renaissance and baroque eras. The great baroque architect Francesco Borromini, who left such a mark on Rome, was himself a Como master craftsman.

Dark but clearly proportioned churches with richly decorated portals and porches, as well as square bell towers on the facades are characteristic of the Lombard Romanesque style. Across in the Garda region, the style reached its zenith in buildings like the magnificent basilica of San Zeno Maggiore in Verona (perhaps the finest Romanesque structure in Northern Italy), San Severo in Bardolino, and San Pietro in Mavino in Sirmione.

Gothic

Originally created in France, the Gothic style first established itself in Lombardy in the middle of the 13th century. While the Italian Gothic adopts the French innovation of the pointed arch, it generally leaves out the exterior flying buttresses, maintaining the solid walls so typical of the Romanesque. The Lombard builders were not too keen on the upwards-striving style of the Gothic, instead preferring classical horizontal lines and broad interior spaces. The gradual transition to Gothic is reflected in the cathe-

Opposite: Roman Verona

Desenzano mosaic

San Zeno Maggiore

San Pietro in Mavino

dral of Santa Maria Matricolare, in Verona. Around lakes Maggiore and Garda, the Gothic style seemed to lack the element of courtly chivalry it so thrived upon. However, in the cathedral in Salò (1453) and the church of San Francesco in Gargnano (13th-century) are both fine examples of the High Gothic style.

Como cathedral

Veronese statue

Renaissance

In around 1400 Florentine builders began to replace the Gothic style by initiating a rebirth of classical motifs and features. Rounded arches, classical columns and great emphasis on the horizontal, achieved for example by cornices, are typical components of the Renaissance style. It gradually made its way across Northern Italy to Lombardy, and Leonardo da Vinci and Bramante were the two artists who helped Renaissance art to flourish here; their students continued the tradition in many buildings and works of art. In the Maggiore region, the most important works dating from the Renaissance period are the facade and choir of Como cathedral, and also Castiglione Olona near Varese, the 'mini-Florence' built in the middle of Lombardy by Cardinal Branda Castiglione.

In Verona the Renaissance flourished, with architects such as Michele Sanmicheli and Fra Giocondo producing some incomparable work including the portal of Salò cathedral and the Loggia del Consiglio (1486–93) in Verona. Many small rural churches built in the Romanesque and Gothic styles were given Renaissance alterations during this period. The facade of the cathedral of San Lorenzo in Lugano is a good example.

A modern facade

Baroque and neoclassical

Two historical highlights of the baroque era are the parish churches of Limone and Riva on Lake Garda. In Varese the Palazzo Estense is another fine example of the style. The neoclassical movement is best exemplified by the Palazzo Oliginati in Como and the Villa dell'Olmo. During the 19th century Milan assumed a leading role in architectural development; the *Risorgimento* and Italian unification meant that very little was built outside the city. Nevertheless, Varese did receive an attractive art nouveau hotel at the turn of the century, the 'Campo dei Fiori'.

20th-century architecture

During the Mussolini era the pompous style associated with Fascism was accompanied by a very sober and oppressive architecture, best exemplified in Como by the Novocomum (1927–29), the Casa del Fascio (1932–36), the Sant'Elia Kindergarten (1936–7) and the Casa Ascheri (1936). The centre of Locarno was redesigned by Mario Cereghini in 1937.

In the Ticino some modern architecture uses local construction materials, such as granite, very successfully. Mario Botta is one of the more famous exponents of the 'Ticino School'; his Cappella Santa Maria degli Angeli, situated 1,567m (5,140ft) above Lake Lugano, is stunning. Botta's residential houses in the Ticino are designed rather like caves; he refers to them himself as *caverne magiche*. Their strict design is based on mathematical forms such as cubes, prisms and cylinders.

Literature and music

One of the most important Italian poets of the 18th century was the Lombard Giuseppe Parini (1729–99), whose elegant satires were later taken up again by Carlo Porta (1775–1821) in his dialect poetry. Among the 19th-century Romantics, Alessandro Manzoni (1785–1873) from Milan occupies a leading position both because of his historical novels such as *The Betrothed*, set on Lake Como and considered to be the most notable novel in Italian literature, and also because of his religious writings.

Of immense importance for the development of European music as a whole was the introduction of the use of hymns in church by Archbishop Ambrose (339–397) of Milan, who even wrote some hymns himself. In more recent times the development of opera has been closely linked with Lombardy, and with Milan's world-famous Teatro alla Scala in particular. The Bergamo-born Gaetano Donizetti (1797–1848) and Giuseppe Verdi (1813–1901), who chose Milan as his home, Amilcare Ponchielli (1834–86) and Umberto Giordano (1867–1948) are just some of the famous local names to be associated with operatic life in Lombardy. Just as immortal is the name of the star conductor of the Scala, Arturo Toscanini (1867–1957), and of cellist Enrico Mainardi (born 1897).

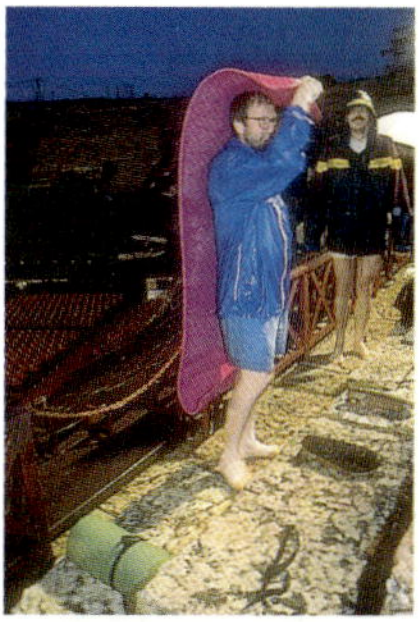

A packed Arena di Verona

Festivals and Folklore

Here are just a few of the many festivals enthusiastically celebrated throughout the year around the Northern Italian lakes. Church festivals and processions are not included here, but naturally they provide yet another chance for a celebration.

Any excuse to celebrate

February **Carnival in Arco**, with processions and colourful masks to scare away winter, evil spirits, etc.

March **Festa di mezza quaresime** in Limone, a one-day-long break in Lent where meat still remains taboo but a great deal of fish and white wine is consumed (especially deep-fried sardines).

April The tiny village of San Giulio near Stresa holds its magnificent **flower festival**. **Good Friday processions** in the villages of Castelletto di Brenzone and Biazza (a few miles south of Malcesine), where the Passion is re-enacted by amateur actors in torchlit olive groves; the **concert and theatre season** opens in Sirmione and Malcesine, with many classical music events; the **Pasqua Musical Arcense** concert festival begins in Arco.

May **San Filippo Neri** in Torri del Benaco, a nocturnal sailing regatta in honour of the local patron saint. The festival reaches its climax when a boat and thousands of floating candles are set alight.

June **Festa popolare del lago di Garda** in Limone, with fish and white wine served up free in the Piazza Garibaldi during the

Verona: Nabucco performance

Sunday celebration. On and around Isola Comacina on the weekend following the feast of St John the Baptist (24 June), the **commemoration of the destruction of the island's city in 1169**, with firework displays symbolising the battle and culminating in a religious procession.

July **Estiva Jazz**, a jazz festival held in the Piazza della Riforma in Lugano, where jazz greats from all over the world meet up. **Musical Festival** in Lugano, a classical music festival where young students have the chance to meet and study with famous professional artists, and master classes are accompanied by a concert programme. **Drodesera Festival** in the romantic old part of Dro, near Riva del Garda, featuring modern dance and theatre as part of the Trentino Festival. **Carnevale del sole** in Salò, a carnival held on the last Saturday in July rather than in the depths of winter.

July/August **Opera Festival in Verona**, the major cultural event of the year in the Garda region, with bus trips organised to the performances from every major town on Lake Garda, and tickets usually included in the price. Remember, however, that stars such as Pavarotti are totally booked out the moment box offices open.

August **International Film Festival in Locarno**, held on the Piazza Grande. The best international film is awarded the *Golden Leopard*. **Settimane Musicale** in Stresa, with concert ensembles performing from all over the world. **Festa di Sant'Ercolano**, a folk festival on 11 and 12 August with fireworks in Toscolano-Maderna; on 15 August the **Palio delle Contrade** is held, a big race in traditional lake boats between the various towns around Lake Garda.

September **Sagra dei Osei**, a whistling and singing contest held on 8 and 9 September in Cisano near Bardolino, in which the competitors have to dress as birds. **Festa dell'Uva** wine festivals held on the last weekend of the month in all wine regions around the lakes, e.g. Bardolino. This is the time to buy vast quantities of very good wine cheaply.

World music in Lugano

Local singer

Food and Drink

Opposite: cutting the Parmesan

Lombard cuisine is as varied as the landscape. The western side of Lake Maggiore belongs to Piedmont, with its truffles, *grissini* and *Barolo*. There are regional specialities here too, of course: a favourite local dish at Lake Orta is *tapulon* (minced donkey braised in red wine), and just as delicious is *trotella alla Savoia* (trout on mushrooms).

Lombardy has some well known traditional favourites, which also have a great influence on the cuisine in neighbouring Ticino: *ossobuco* (sliced veal braised in white wine), for instance, the unmistakeably yellow *risotto alla milanese*, or the *costoletta alla milanese*, mentioned in a Lombard cookbook dated 1134 as *lombolos cum panitio*, discovered in the 19th century by the Austrian field-marshal Radetsky and promptly introduced to the Austrian capital as the *Wiener Schnitzel*.

Local seasoning

A speciality of the Varesotto is *faraona alla Valcuvia*, partridge Valcuvia-style, formerly baked in a soft clay container. Around Verona the *risotto* comes into its own. And for some real Lombard home cooking, why not try a very filling *cazzoeula* (pork stew)?

A ubiquitous dish, particularly in the more mountainous areas, is maize pudding or *polenta*. In restaurants it is often served with rabbit or as *pancetta con polenta* (cured bacon with polenta), but the locals often eat it on its own or with cheese. Maize was only introduced to the region from America in the 17th century; prior to that the staple of the mountain folk was chestnut porridge.

Fish variation

Fish is of course an integral part of the cuisine around the Italian lakes. *Agonia alla Comasca* (baked and marinated shad), *Anguilla del pescatore* (stewed eel), *lavarelli al vino bianco* (white fish in white wine), *pesce in gelatina* (fish in aspic) and *suppa di pesce alla tremezzina* (fish soup) are just a few of the numerous fish specialities. A typical Lake Como delicacy is *curadura* (salted and dried shad), a former 'poor man's meal' which has now becomes something of a gourmet speciality. The delicate Lake Garda trout known as *Carpione* should definitely be sampled too.

Light lunch

As far as desserts are concerned one of the best ways to wind up a meal Lombard-style is with a *panettone* (yeast cake) from Milan. Another option is to order the wickedly rich *tiramisú*.

Italian cheese is quite delicious, and *gorgonzola* or *bel paese* are always a good bet. Lombard cheese include *grana* (better known to us as Parmesan), *mascarpone* and *stracchino*. The *formaggini* (fresh cheeses flavoured with oil and hot paprika) from Ticino are particularly good; *robiola* comes from the Valsassina and soft *gaprini* comes

Wine comes in a variety of forms

All this talk of cheese naturally leads on to wine. Lombardy is not one of the most important wine regions of Italy, but its reds are particularly good. Top-quality wines come from Piedmont, e.g. *Barolo* (a heavy red). In Ticino the top wine is the ruby-red *Merlot*. Over near Lake Garda, more famous names appear: *Bardolino, Valpolicella* and *Soave* are all grown around Verona, and all delicious. The purple-coloured *Bardolino* comes in varying degrees of quality, and can be tasted all over the place.

One very popular grape in the region south of Lake Garda is the *Trebbiano*, used to make an excellent dry white. A light, fizzy rosé is grown in the Valetnesi region north of Desenzano, and two more fine wines worthy of mention are the heavy white *Tocai del Garda* and the very versatile *Recioto* from the Val Policella. Naturally, a *vino della casa* can always be ordered; they are usually dry, light and 'honest'. One very good one is *Nostrano*, from Ticino.

Downtown Ascona

Here are some restaurants from some of the most popular places mentioned in this guide. They are listed according to three categories: **$$$** = expensive, **$$** = moderate and **$** = inexpensive.

Arona

$$Trattoria Campagna, Via Vergante 12, tel: 0322-57294. Rustic surroundings, very good Italian cuisine.

Ascona

$$Da Ivo, Via Collegio 141, tel: 093-351031. Good cooking in a pleasant environment.

Como cakes and café

Bardolino

$$$Taverna Scalchi, Cisano, Via Peschiera 40, tel: 045-721 1917. First-class gourmet restaurant; **$$Bardolino**, Piazza Matteotti 14, tel: 045-721 0043. Venetian cuisine; **$Al Commercio**, Via Solferino 1, tel: 045-721 1183. Simple and good.

Como

$$$Ristorante Raimondi dell'Hotel Villa Flori, Via Cenobbio 10, tel: 031-573105. Elegant restaurant in attractive villa, the noodles with shrimps are very good; **$$Sant'Anna 1907**, Via Turati 1/3, tel: 031-505266. Grilled swordfish is the speciality in this family-run restaurant; **$Tipica Trattoria**, Via Pannilani, tel: 031-261080. Very good seafood.

Desenzano del Garda

$$$Cavallino, Via Murachette 29, tel: 030-912 1485. Top address for gourmets, also does regional dishes.

Garda
$$$Locanda di San Vigilio, Punta San Vigilio, tel: 045-725 6688. Elegant, delicious, expensive; **$$Stafolet**, Via Poiano 12, tel: 045-725 5427. Excellent cooking in quiet surroundings; **$Al Pontesel**, Via Monte Baldo 71, tel: 045-725 5419. Pizza and pasta.

Cooling off at Garda

Gardone Riviera
$$$Villa Fiordaliso, tel: 0365-20158. This pink villa was Mussolini's mistress's last place of abode, and today is renowned for its seafood dishes.

Gargnano
$$$La Tortuga, Via XXIV Maggio 5, tel: 0365-71251. One of the best and also most expensive gourmet restaurants in the region, reservations essential.

Iseo
$$$Le Maschere, Vicolo della Pergola 7, tel: 030-982 1542. Regional specialities and classic dishes, also excellent wines; **$Il Volto**, Via Manica 2, tel: 030-981462. A small *osteria* with a lot of tradition.

Laveno
$$Lo Scoiattolo, Via Monteggia, tel: 0332-668253. Classic Italian cuisine, summer veranda.

Lazise
$$It Porticciolo, Lungolago Marconi, tel: 045-758 0254, regional cuisine; **$La Forgia**, Lungolago Marconi, tel: 045-758 0287, speciality grilled fish.

Lecco
$$$Ristorante al Porticciolo, Via Valsecchi 5/7, tel: 0341-498103. A gourmet restaurant that's difficult to forget; **$$$Antica Osteria Enoteca Casa di Lucia**, Via Lucia 27, tel: 0341-494594. Excellent Italian cuisine in an old villa in the town centre.

Late night in Locarno

Limone sul Garda
$$Gemma, Piazza Garibaldi 10, tel: 0365-954014. Good pasta dishes.

Locarno
$$Trattoria da Luigi, Via Dogana Vecchia, tel: 093-319746. Ticino cuisine in pleasant environment; **$$Ca'Nostra**, Brione s/Minusio, tel: 093-335852. Excellent Ticino cuisine served on terrace with panoramic view; **$Grott'al Capon**, Brione s/Minusio, tel: 093-331012. Idyllic grotto north of Locarno with good local cuisine.

Lugano
$$$Bianchi, Via Pessina 3, tel: 091-228479. Oldest restaurant in town, with much *grandezza*; **$$La Tineva**, Via dei Giomi 2, tel: 091-235219. Delicious Ticino cooking; **$Sayonnara**, Soave 4, tel: 091-220170. Ticino specialities.

Malcesine
$$$Del Park Hotel Querceto, loc Campiano, tel: 045-740 0344. Regional cuisine in elegant surroundings; **$$La Toresela**, loc Cassone, Via Chiesa 9. tel: 045-740 0241. Pasta and seafood; **$$Da Mamma Ida**, loc Val di Sogno, tel: 045-740 0216. 200 pasta specialities, a paradise for noodle-lovers; **$Pizzeria San Remo**, loc Campagnola, tel: 045-740 0239. Pizza served from clay ovens.

Riva
$$$Vecchia Riva, Via Bastione 3, tel: 0464-555061. Excellent seafood; **$$$Restel de Fer**, Via Restel de Fer, tel: 0464-553481. Lake Garda fish specialities served to folklore performances; **$$Al Volt**, Via Fiume 73, tel: 0464-552570. Nice family-run establishment; **$San Marco**, Via Roma 20, tel: 0464-554477. International cuisine.

Dining in Stresa

Salò
$$Trattoria La Campagnola, Via Brunati 11, tel: 0365-22153. Family-run, home-grown ingredients too; **$Antica Trattoria Nando**, 1km (½ mile) out of town in Campoverde, tel: 0365-40027. Good grilled food.

Sirmione
$$$Vecchia Lugana, Lugana, Via Verona 71, tel: 030-919012. One of the top addresses on the lake, regularly praised by food writers; **$$$Rucola**, Vicolo Strentelle 7, tel: 030-916326. Superb cooking; **$$Ancora d'Oro**, loc Colombara, Via d'Aquisto, tel: 030-990 4696. Seafood specialities; **$Osteria del Pescatore**, Via Piana 24, tel: 030-916216. Cheap restaurant in the old part of town.

Stresa
$$$Piemontese, Via Mazzini 25, tel: 0323-30235. The very best Piedmontese cuisine, delicious and expensive; **$$$La Scuderia**, Villa Pallavicino, tel: 0323-31895. Delicious Italian food; **$$L'Emiliano**, Corso Italia 52, tel: 0323-31396. Intimate, elegant restaurant with local cheese specialities; **$$Del Pescatore**, Vicvolo del Poncivo 3, tel: 0323-31986. Good and inexpensive seafood.

Torbole
$$$Da Sergio, loc Coe, tel: 0464-505301. Pasta and seafood in romantic surroundings; **$$$Piccolo Mondo**, Via Matteotti 7, tel: 0464-505271. Great Trentino cuisine,

the speciality is a menu consisting entirely of apple dishes; **$$Al Pescatore**, Via Segantini 11, tel: 0464-505236. Seafood served in the open air; **$$la Terrazza**, Via Benaco 14, tel: 0464-506083. Seafood right beside the lake; **$Aurora**, Via Matteotti 2, tel: 0464-505311. Rustic, inexpensive; **$Cin Cin**, Via Matteotti 38, tel: 0464-505238. Good rice and pizza dishes.

Toscolano-Maderno
$$Rustichell, loc Maclino, tel: 0365-642610. Food served on terrace with view of the lake; **$Milani**, Via Bianchi 7, tel: 0365-641042. The speciality here is called *Filetti di San Pietro*.

Varese
$$Ristorante Lago Maggiore, Via Carobbio 19, tel: 0331-231183. Finest Italian cooking, especially the seafood.

Verbania
$$Il Torchio, Via Manzoni 20, tel: 0323-503352. Good Italian food, Piedmontese specialities; **$Pizzeria Laguna Blu**, Piazza Matteotti 16, tel: 0323-404289.

Verona
$$$Arche, Via Arche Scaligere 6, tel: 045-800 7415. Closed Sunday and Monday noon, first-class restaurant; **$$$Il Desco**, Via Dietro San Sebastiano 7, tel: 045-595358. Recommended by all leading Italian food writers; **$$Maffei**, Piazza Erbe 38, tel: 045-801 0015. Scampi with asparagus cream is the speciality here; **$$I Dodici Apostoli**, Corticella San Marco 3, tel: 045-596999. Try the Venetian liver, king prawns or rabbit; **$Osteria La Fontanina**, loc. Santo Stefano, tel: 045-913305. Cheap and cosy.

Comings and goings in Verona

High season on Lake Garda

Active Holidays

Angling

Official angling licences have to be procured. They are valid throughout Italy for three months, and cost L60,000. The respective local authorities then issue angling permits. Fishing without a permit is subject to a high fine. More information is available from tourist authorities.

Hiking and climbing

The mountains around Lake Garda are served by well-marked paths and mountain huts (*rifugio*), and include the Monte Baldo high-level route and Monte Pizzocolo above the western shore. The mountains of Ticino and around-Lake Como are also easily accessible; around Lake Maggiore the routes are often more difficult to find. Hiking maps can be obtained from the local tourist offices (ATP).

The centre of mountain climbing in the Garda region is Arco, a few miles from the northern tip of the lake. The mountains around Maggiore provide climbing fans with routes of varying degrees of difficulty. Near Como, the paradise for climbers is definitely the Grigna, north of Lecco; the town itself also has a renowned climbing school that does several courses in mountaineering.

Ready for the road

Cycling

The Italians have always been very keen cyclists, and numerous *Girini* can be seen around the lakes, primarily at weekends. Bicycles *(biciclette)* can be hired in Ticino at any major rail station. There is a signposted cycle route from Bellinzona to Ascona. The best routes for cycles are the tiny ones between the lakes, or the flat area south of Lake Garda in particular. Mountain bikes can also be hired in most places, but remember that a lot of mountain roads are closed between November and mid-April. A tip for the less ambitious: the cable car from Malcesine on Lake Garda up to Monte Baldo also takes mountain bikes, saving an exhausting ascent and providing you with a superb trip back down.

Golf

Golfers will find excellent courses in Ascona (18 holes), Lugano (18), Carimate (18), Lanzo d'Intelvi (9), Montorfano (18), Appiano Gentile (18), Cassina Rizzardi (36), Ca'degli Ulivi (18) and Sommacampagna (near Desenzano, 18).

Hang-gliding

For courses in this at Lugano, the school to contact is the Scuola Volo delta Lugano, tel: 092-822487. Near Lake Garda, the cable railways from Malcesine up to Monte Baldo and from Prada to Costabella take gliders up to 1,800m (5,900ft), allowing the opportunity to take at least two flights a day. The local hang-gliding school in the Garda region is Deltaland, loc. Platano di Caprino Veronese, tel: 045-7241263.

Happy landings

Riding

The countryside around the Northern Italian lakes is ideal for riding trips. Near Garda, the best riding routes are in the hilly country inland from Garda itself, along the slopes of Monte Baldo, or the river meadows along the Moncio. In the Maggiore region, there are riding schools in Losone (near Locarno), Quartino (near Magadino), Angera, Ghirla (Varesotto), Bodio (Lake Varese) and Magreglio and Canzo (both on Lake Como).

Sky-diving

For an exhilarating aerial view of Lake Maggiore, why not fall out of a plane belonging to either the Cardada Cimetti in Locarno (tel: 093-672651) or the Scuola Volo Libero Lugano (tel: 091-525821)?

Water sports

Windsurfing is available on Lakes Maggiore and Como, but nowhere is more popular than the northern part of Lake Garda, around Torbole. Here the surfers get blown southwards by the *Tramuntana* in the mornings and then up the lake again in the evenings by the *Ora*. In the summer months there are sometimes so many windsurfers around that ordinary swimming becomes almost impossible; there again, the water in the southern part is much warmer for bathing anyway. All the lakes have facilities for every conceivable kind of other water sport including diving, water-skiing and sailing; the larger resorts have schools.

Ideal winds off Torbole

OSTERI
Antica Osteria Vacchini
DA CARLO
tipico giardino ticinese
typisches tessiner garten

Getting There

Opposite: getting around Ascona

By Plane

For Lake Como and Lake Maggiore, the most convenient port of entry is Milan. British Airways and Alitalia each operate 4 flights a day to Milan-Linate Airport from London Heathrow. Direct flights from the US arrive at Milan-Malpensa Airport. Visitors from the UK to the Lake Garda region are advised to fly to Verona; British Airways operates 2 flights a day from London Gatwick. There are no direct flights to Verona from the US, so visitors might consider flying via London. Alternatively, Verona can be reached in a more roundabout manner (a train journey or a very expensive taxi ride) from either Venice or Milan.

By train

If travelling direct from the UK, the most convenient place to head for is Milan. Take the Eurostar to Gard du Nord in Paris, then cross to Gare du Lyon for overnight services to Milan through the Simplon Tunnel. Milan is connected by rail to Lake Maggiore, Varese, Como and Bergamo, as well as Brescia, the southern tip of Lake Garda and Verona which are all on the main line to Venice. If arriving from Germany or Austria, another possibility for Lake Garda is via the Brenner Pass, and down to Rovereto or Verona, each of which have direct bus connections to every resort on the lake. For the Maggiore and Como region, there are also hourly trains via Switzerland along the so-called 'Gotthard line'.

Train spotters

By Car

Northern Italy is well connected to the rest of Europe by motorway, but it's worth remembering that if you arrive via Switzerland you need to buy a special *vignette* (valid one year, price Sf40).

Drivers must always carry a driving licence, the car registration documents and insurance certificate. Breakdown service is usually free of charge for members of automobile clubs. Seat-belts are compulsory in Italy. Never leave anything in the car which might attract thieves – not even for a few moments. Also, remember that the fines for traffic offences in Italy (parking, speed limits, etc) are high.

The following speed limits apply to motor traffic in Italy unless otherwise indicated: 50kmph (30mph) in built-up areas, 90kmph (55mph) on country roads, and 130kmph (75mph) on motorways (*autostrada*). Speed limits are often lowered at weekends or on public holidays. Police checks have become much stricter in recent times, and excessive speed as well as excessive alcohol consumption can cost motorists their licence – this also applies to foreign drivers.

Getting Around

Skirting Lake Garda

By Car

Without a car it's virtually impossible to see the best that the lakes have to offer. Renting a car is probably cheaper than bringing your own, and there is no shortage of fly-drive packages, where cars can be collected on arrival. Alternatively, both international and local car hire firms are represented in the major centres.

Driving along the narrow, winding mountain roads requires care and attention. Remember that the car nearest the mountain has priority. It is customary to use the horn to warn that you are about to overtake and to warn of your presence on a blind bend. Many of the roads in the area, particularly the one along the western shore of Lake Garda, disappear into tunnels. Here, dipped headlights must be used.

By Train

Near the lakes themselves, the following connections are possible: Locarno–Luino–Laveno–Sesto Calende; Simplon–Stresa–Sesto Calende; Laveno–Varese–Milan; Como–Milan; Como–Lecco; and Milan–Lecco–Colico. As far as tickets are concerned, keep an eye out for the various special offers available from the Swiss (SBB) and the Italian railways (FS). For connections from Milan to Lake Garda, remember that the fast express trains don't stop at Peschiera, Sirmione or Desenzano.

Getting to the other side

By Bus

There are very good bus networks in Switzerland and Italy, and reaching destinations usually poses no problems at all. The local tourist offices can provide timetables and general information.

By Boat

One of the best and most relaxing ways of seeing the lakes is from the deck of a steamer. All major towns on the Italian lakes have ferry connections for passengers, and a number of towns are linked by car ferry as well: Verbania–Laveno on Lake Maggiore; Menaggio–Bellagio–Varenna and Cadenabbia–Bellagio–Varenna on Lake Como; and Maderno–Torri del Benaco on Lake Garda). The Maggiore and Lugano steamers cross the border between Italy and Switzerland, so the usual border procedures apply. The larger vessels have on-board restaurants. For a trip along the full length of Lake Garda, from Desenzano to Riva, allow around four and a half hours.

Cruises are a regular feature during the summer months, and disco ships are also common. Genuine old-fashioned paddle steamers are still used by some operators.

A place for children, too

Facts for the Visitor

Travel documents

Visitors from European Union countries require either a passport or identification card to enter Italy. Holders of passports from most other countries do not usually require visas for a period not exceeding three months.

Customs

There have been practically no customs limits for nationals of EU member states since 1993. The following are just rough guidelines: 800 cigarettes, 200 cigars, 1kg of tobacco, 90 litres of wine.

Currency regulations

Unlimited amounts of foreign currency and Italian lire may be brought in and out of Italy, but need to be declared if the sum exceeds L20 million.

Tourist information

Here are the addresses of the Italian Tourist Office (ENIT): **UK**: 1 Princes Street, London W1, tel: 0171-408 1254. **US**: 630 Fifth Avenue, Suite 1565, New York NY 10111, tel: (212) 245-4822.

When in Italy, contact the APT (Azienda di Promozione Turistica): APT Verona, Via Montanari 14, 37100 Verona, tel: 045-800 6997; APT Garda/Trentino, Giardini di Porta Orientale 8, 38066 Riva del Garda, tel: 0464-554444; APT Como, Piazza Cavour 17, 22100 Como, tel: 031 262091/269712; APT del Varesotto, Viale Ippodromo 9, 21100 Varese; APT del Lago Maggiore, Via Principe Tomaso 70/72, 28049 Stresa, tel: 0323-30150. APT Bergamo, 20 Viale Vittorio Emanuele II, tel: 035 213185/242226. In addition, towns and many villages in the lakes area have a tourist information centre, usually centrally located.

Currency and exchange

The unit of currency in Italy is the lira (abbreviated to Lit. or L), which comes in 5, 10, 20, 50, 100, 200 and 500 lire coins, and 1,000, 2,000, 5,000, 10,000, 50,000 and 100,000 lire notes. Foreign and Italian currency not exceeding 20 million lire in value may be brought in and out of the country; larger sums need to be declared.

Eurocheques can be cashed up to a maximum value of 300,000 lire at banks with the EC symbol. Most credit cards, including Visa, Access and American Express, are accepted in hotels, restaurants and shops and for air and train tickets and cash at any bank. All the larger towns in the region have automatic bank tellers ('Bancomat').

Tipping

This is expected, despite all-inclusive prices (approximately 10 percent).

Bills and receipts

Not only the Italians themselves but also foreign tourists are expected to have receipts (*ricevuta fiscale*) made out by restaurants, hotels, car repair workshops, etc, listing services rendered plus the correct amount of Italian VAT (IVA) and to keep them on their person for possible checks by the Italian fiscal authorities. Failure to furnish receipts can often result in a stiff fine.

Opening times

Generally, shops are open on weekdays from 9am–7.30pm with a lunch break from 1–3.30pm. Many shops are closed on Saturday and Monday mornings.

Banks: Monday to Friday 8.30am–1.30pm; some also open in the afternoon from 2.45pm–3.45pm. Money can be exchanged at weekends in the railway stations and airports of the larger cities.

Museum opening hours vary considerably, and the times stated in this book are subject to change. State-owned museums are generally open daily from 9am–2pm, and 9am–1pm on Sunday and public holidays. They are often closed on Monday. Note: some state-owned and municipal museums allow free admission to visitors under 18 and over 60 years of age.

Churches are usually closed around lunchtime, roughly from noon–4pm.

Filling Stations, apart from those on the motorways, are closed at lunchtime and on Sunday and public holidays. Some have cash-operated automatic pumps.

Beachware

Souvenirs

Most souvenirs are of the gastronomic variety, with finest-quality olive oil, cheese, truffles, sausages, honey, wine and *grappa* usually topping the list. Bargains can also be had at flea markets in the larger towns; try to avoid the innumerable boutiques in the tourist resorts. Antiques markets are also a good place to buy special items cheaply. Ask at the local tourist information outlet about where and when they are held.

Public holidays

1 January, 6 January (Epiphany), Easter Sunday, Easter Monday, 25 April (National Day of Liberation), 1 May, Whit Sunday, 15 August (Assumption of the Virgin, ferragosto), 1 November, 8 December (Immaculate Conception), and 25 and 26 December (Christmas).

In addition, many businesses close at some time during August and whole towns tend to close when a major festival is in progress.

Post haste

Postal services

Main post offices in major towns are open all day, some as late as 7pm, otherwise the hours are Monday to Saturday 8am to 1.30pm. Stamps are sold at post offices as well as at bars and tobacconists; look for the white letter T on a blue background.

Telephone

Post-modern phones

Calls can be made from phone centres run by the phone company TELECOM (not in post offices). Coin-operated phones take L100, L200 and L500 coins and also gettoni (phone tokens), which can be purchased either over the counter or from special machines. A phone card (scheda telefonica) is a more convenient way of telephoning; these come in L5,000 or L10,000 versions and are available from tobacconists or from TELECOM offices.

There is direct dialling to most countries. Within the country, use a three-number code which is different for each city. If calling Italy from abroad, dial 0039 then the area code number, dropping the inital 0. From Italy, dial 00 followed by the international code (44 for the UK, 1 for the US) then the area code number (dropping the initial 0 for calls to the UK). For information, dial 184.

AT&T: 172-1011, Sprint: 172-1877, MCI: 172-1022.

Hours ahead

Time

Italy is six hours ahead of US Eastern Standard Time and one hour ahead of Greenwich Mean Time.

Voltage

Usually 220v – the voltage is printed on the bulbs. Safety plugs cannot always be used. Specialist shops can provide adaptors *(spina di adattamento)*; however, owners of American appliances will need a transformer.

Nude Sunbathing

Stripping off completely is not allowed. The 'monokini' is largely tolerated these days, but there are no nudist beaches on any of the lakes.

Crime

The lakes are relatively free of crime, but visitors should still take the usual precautions: don't leave any valuables inside your car, always lock the vehicle when you leave it, and leave your cash in the hotel safe. When out walking in big towns and cities keep a close eye on your cameras and handbags.

The summer crush

Medical

With Form E111 from the Department of Health and Social Security, UK visitors are entitled to reciprocal medical treatment in Italy. There are similar arrangements for other members of EU countries. It may nevertheless be advisable to take out insurance for private treatment in case of accident. Holiday insurance policies and private patients schemes are recommended for non-EU visitors.

In case of minor ailments, chemists (*farmacie*) are well stocked with medicines, often sold without prescription. Farmacie, which are normally open Monday to Friday 9am–1pm and 4–7pm, are identified by a sign displaying a green cross on a white background. For other times, the address of the nearest emergency chemist will be posted in the window.

Emergencies

Emergency Assistance (Ambulance, fire, police), tel: 113.
Police Immediate Action, tel: 112.
Breakdown service, tel: 116.
Emergency medical assistance, tel: 118.

Winding down

Accommodation

Whether you feel like sleeping in a 17th-century villa, a *casa rustico* or out on a campsite, Ticino, Lombardy and Piedmont all have a huge variety of accommodation possibilities to suit every taste.

On Lake Maggiore, the luxury hotels tend to be on the Swiss side, around Verbania, while smaller, family-run hotels are mostly located on the eastern shore. There is luxury in abundance, too, on Lake Lugano and around Como, and the hotels are usually magnificent old villas surrounded by extensive parks. Alongside these five-star establishments there are also numerous medium-priced ones that offer cable TV, swimming pools and air conditioning. Around Lake Garda there are less of the luxurious five-star hotels that one sees elsewhere.

Generally speaking, the nearer a lake a hotel is, the more expensive the accommodation. Cheaper logdings can be found in the towns and villages of the hinterland, away from the lakes, where one can find not only hotels but also pensions and rooms let out by farmers (*agroturismo*). Campsites are usually right beside the lakes (the ones inland are a lot cheaper and quieter), and generally have all modern conveniences even though they can often be overcrowded in the summer months.

Anyone keen to book a holiday house can organise anything from a *casa rustica* to an enormous villa. More information can be obtained from the tourist offices.

Hotel selection

Here is a selection of hotels from some of the most popular centres. They are listed according to three categories: **$$$** = expensive, **$$** moderate and **$** = inexpensive.

Ascona
$$$Ascovilla, Via Albarelle, tel: 093-350252. Four-star hotel surrounded by subtropical park; **$$$Romantik**, Piazza G Motta 35, tel: 093-791 0282. Ticino patrician residence with attractive inner courtyard and good restaurant.

Bardolino
$$Du Lac, Via S Cristina, tel: 045-721 1917. Has its own beach and a fine restaurant; **$Al Parco**, Via Fosse 20, tel: 045-721 0039. Centrally located, not all that quiet.

Bellagio
$$$Grand Hotel Villa Serbelloni, tel: 031-950216, fax: 951229. Romantic luxury hotel in old villa right on Lake Como; **$$Fiorini – da Piero**, tel: 031-950392. Good, cheap and comfortable; **$La Pergola**, 031-950263. Simple, clean establishment, family-run.

Villa d'Este in Como

Brissago
$$$Villa Caesar, tel: 093-652766. A noble and elegant establishment right beside the lake, surrounded by subtropical vegetation.

Palace Hotel, Como

Como
$$$Villa d'Este, Montorfano, tel: 031-200200. A 16th-century villa with five-star luxury; **$$$Palace Hotel**, Lungolario Trieste 16, tel: 031-303303. Four-star establishment by the lake and near the cathedral; **$$Metropole Suisse**, Piazza Cavour 19, tel: 031-269444. Good reasonably-priced hotel in the centre.

Desenzano del Garda
$$$Lido International, Via Tommaso dal Mulin 43, tel: 030-914 1027, fax: 914 3736. A very good hotel; **$$City**, Via Nazario Sauro 29, tel: 030-991 1704, fax: 991 2837. Nice town hotel with all mod cons, quiet; **$Principe**, Via Grigollo 20, tel: 030-912 1485. Good for a night.

Guarding Garda

Garda
$$$Du Parc, Via Marconi 3, 045-725 5343. Beautifully situated in a grove of palm trees next to the lake; **$$Flora**, Via Madrina 4, 045-725 5348. Includes sauna, swimming pool and tennis courts, very friendly service; **$Marco Polo**, Via dei Cipressi, 045-725 5335. Cheap and comfortable.

Gardone Riviera
$$$Grand Hotel Gardone Riviera, Lungolago, tel: 0365-20261, fax: 22695. Luxury establishment with nearly a century of tradition; **$$Bellevue**, Via Zarnadelli 81, tel: 0365-290088, fax: 290080. Very comfortable; **$San Michele**, Via S Michele 9, tel: 0365-20703. A good inexpensive place to stay.

Gargnano
$$$Villa Giulia, Viale Rimebranza, tel: 0365-71022, fax: 72744. Quiet location, next to lake; **$$Europa**, Via Repubblica 38, tel: 0365-71191. Modern establishment, very comfortable.

Laveno
$$Moderno, tel: 0332-668373, reasonably-priced, medium-category hotel.

Limone sul Garda
$$$Park Hotel Imperial, Via Tamas 10, tel: 0365-95491, fax: 954382. Five-star luxury, beauty cures, fitness studios; **$$Cristina**, Via Tamas 20, tel: 0365-954641, fax: 954139. Nice affordable lodgings; **$Sole**, Lungolago Maconi 26, tel: 0365-954055. Centrally situated, cheap.

Locarno
$$$La Palma au Lac, Viale Verbano 29, Locarno Muralto, tel: 093-330971. Four-star hotel with piazza and grandezza, right next to the lake; **$$Remorino Minusio**, Via Verbano 29, tel: 331033. Ticino charm and lake view.

Lugano
$$$Grand Hotel Villa Castagnola, Viale Castagnola 31, tel: 091-512213, fax: 527271. Beautifully situated by the lake, five-star luxury; **$$$Hotel de la Paix**, Via Cattori 18, tel: 091-542332, fax: 54951. Elegant, grand hotel; **$$Meister**, Via San Salvatore 11, tel: 091-541412, fax: 548513. Good hotel, centrally located.

Luino
$$$Camin, Via Dante 35, tel: 0332-530118, fax: 537226. Elegant hotel surrounded by park at the centre of town.

Malcesine
$$$Park Hotel Eden, Via Gardesana Navene, tel: 045-657 0130, fax: 740 1160. For the very wealthy; **$$Reporter**, Viale Roma 40, tel: 045-740 0560, fax: 657 0114. Exclusive establishment right next to the lake; **$Lago di Garda**, Piazza Matteotti 1, tel: 045-740 0246. Centrally located, not the quietest of places.

Morcote
$Carina-Carlton, Via Cantonale, tel: 091-691131, fax: 691929. Small and comfortable hotel.

Riva del Garda
$$$Sole, Piazza 3 Novembre 35, tel: 0464-552686, fax: 552811. A venerable hotel; **$$Bellavista**, Piazza C Battisti 4, tel: 0464-552344, fax: 552138; **$Bastione**, Via Bastione 19, tel: 0464-552652. Cheap lodgings for gourmets.

Salò
$$$Laurin, Viale Landi 9, tel: 0365-22022, fax: 22382. Stylish art nouveau hotel right next to the lake; **$$Barbarano al Lago**, Via Privati Bravi, tel: 0365-20324, fax: 20883. Nice lake hotel; **$Panoramica**, Via del Panorama 28, tel: 0365-41435, fax: 521210. Appropriately-named, a short way outside town.

Sirmione
$$$Villa Cortine Palace Hotel, Via Grotte 12, tel: 030-990 5890, fax: 916390. Live like a prince in this luxury neoclassical palazzo; **$$$Grand Hotel Terme**, Viale Marconi 7, tel: 030-916261, fax: 916568. Five-star luxury, with its own thermal baths and superb grounds; **$$$Sirmione**, Piazza Castello 19, tel: 030-916331, fax: 916558. Very

Locarno Casino

Service with a smile

Opposite: Val Veddasca houses

good service; **$$Golf et Suisse**, Via Condominio 2, tel: 030-990 4188, fax: 916304. Modern family hotel with its own beach; **$Benaco**, Via Colombare, tel: 030-919103, fax: 990 4201. A good place to see Sirmione on the cheap.

Stresa elegance

Stresa
$$$Des Iles Borromées, Lungolago Umberto I 31, tel: 0323-30431, fax: 32405. Elegant luxury hotel with much *grandezza*, in beautiful grounds; **$$Lido 'La Perla Nera'**, Lido di Carciano, tel: 0323-33611. Nice family-run establishment in a park.

Torbole
$$$Clubhotel La Vela, Via Strada Granda 2, tel: 0464-505940. Popular with wealthy windsurfers; **$$Villa Verde**, Via Foci del Sarca 15, tel: 0464-505274. A quiet family-run establishment; **$Villa Clara**, Via Matteotti 13, tel: 0464-505141. Cheap and comfortable.

Torri del Benaco
$$Gardesana, Piazza Calderini 20, tel: 045-722 5411, fax: 722 5771. Traditional hotel right next to the harbour, with an excellent restaurant; **$Belvedere**, Via per Albisano, tel: 045-722 5088. Quiet and friendly.

Toscolano-Maderno
$$$Benaco, Lungolago Zanardelli 27, tel: 0365-641110. Elegant and noble, in a magnificent park right next to the lake; **$$Piccolo Paradiso**, Cecina-Messaga, tel: 0365-643080. Cheap apartments, ideal for a family holiday; **$Sole**, Via Promontorio 7, tel: 0365-641335, simple hotel for those on a low budget.

Varese waiter

Varese
$$Il Sole di Ranco, Ranco (Varese), tel: 0331-976507, fax: 976620, modern apartment hotel with the best food for miles around, and definitely worth a detour.

Verbania
$$$Majestic, Via Vittorio Veneto 32, tel: 0323-504305, fax: 556379, luxury hotel with attractive grounds, right next to the lake; **$$San Gotthardo**, Piazza Imbarcadero, tel: 0323-504465, good and reasonably-priced hotel.

Verona
$$$Due Torri Hotel Baglioni, Piazza S Ananstasia 4, tel: 045-595044, fax: 800 4130. The most traditional five-star hotel in the city; **$$Giulietta e Romeo**, Via Tre Marchetti 3, tel: 800 3554, fax: 801 0862. Very comfortable, not only for lovers; **$Garda**, Via Gardesana 35, tel: 890 3877 Well situated between the city and Lake Garda.

Index

Abbadia Lariana 46
Abbazia di
Maguzzano 66
accommodation 99
Anfo 71
Angera 23
architecture 79–80
Arco 58
Arcumeggia 25
Argegno 41
Arona 22
Ascona 17

Bagolino 71
Bardolino 62
Baveno 20
Bellagio 44–5
Bellano 48
Bergamo 49–50
Bissone 31
Boat Museum 42
Borghetto di Valeggio
sul Mincio 64–5
Borromean Islands 21
Brissago 17–18
Brissago Islands 18
Buco dei Carpi 45

Campagna 24
Cannero Riviera 19
Cannobio 18
Capo di Ponte 54
Capolago 31
Carate 40–1
Carona 30
Casteletto 60
Castelli di Cannero 19
Castelseprio 27
Castiglione Olona 27
Cernobbio 40
Civenna 45
climate 7
Colico 48
Colma del Piano 44
Como 35–8
Castello Baradello 38
Cathedral 36
San Fedele 37
Sant' Abbondio 38
Museo Archeologico
Artistico 37
Tempio Voltano 38
Torre di Porta
Vittoria 38
Villa dell'Olmo 38
Corenno Plinio 48
cuisine 85
Custoza 64

Desenzano del Garda ..66

Economy 9
Eremo Monastery 61
Esino Lario 48

Festivals 82–3
flora and fauna 8

Gandria 32
Garda 61
Garda Safari Park 62
Gardone Riviera 68
Gargnano 68–9
Gavirate 25
geology 6
Gravedona 42
Grigna, Le 46, 48
Grotte di Catullo 63
Gurro 19

Idro 71
Intelvi Valley 41
Iseo 53–4
Isola Comacina 41

Lake Como 39–48
Lake Garda 55–69
Lake Idro 70–1
Lake Iseo 51–4
Lake Ledro 71
Lake Lugano 28–34
Lake Maggiore 14–24
Lake Orta 22
Lake Valvestino 70
Lake Varese 25–6
language 8–9
Laveno 24
Lazise 62
Lecco 45
Lenno 41
Lierna 47
Limone sul Garda 69
Locarno 16–17
Lonato 66
Lovere 51
Lugano 28–30
Luino 24

Maccagno 24
Madonna della
Coronna 61
Madonna del Frassino .64
Madonna del Ghisallo .45
Madonna di
Monte Castello 69
Malcesine 58–9
Malnate 27
Mandello del Lario 47
Manerba del Garda 67
Marmitte dei Giganti ...58
Melide 30

Menaggio 34, 42
Mendrisio 32
Mezzegra 41
Moniga del Garda 67
Monte Baldo 59–60
Monte Brione 58
Monte Generoso 30–1
Monte Grona 34
Monte Isola 52–3
Monte Lema 24
Monte Luppia 60
Monte Mottarone 22
Monte San Primo 45
Monte Tremezzo 34
Monte Zeda 20
Morcote 30

Orrido Sant'Anna 19
Orta San Giulio 22
Ossuccio 41
Osteno 33–4

Parco Giardino
Sigurtà 65
Peschiera del Garda 62
Pieve 69
Piona Abbey 48
Ponte Visconteo 65
Porlezza 33
Porto Valtravaglia 24
Punta San Vigilio 60
Puria 33

Riva 57–8
Riva San Vitale 31–2
Rocca di Caldè 24

Sacro Monte
(Varese) 26–7
Salò 67
San Martino della
Battaglia 65
San Pietro al Monte 46
San Zeno
di Montagna 60
Santa Caterina
del Sasso 23
Santa Maria del
Carmine 67
Santa Maria
delleNeve 52
Santuario della Madonna
della Caravina 33
Sarnico 51
Sassa Gordona 41
Sesto Calende 22
Sirmione 63
Solferino 65
Stresa 21
Swiss Minature 30

Torbole 58
Torno 43–4
Torri del Benaco 60
Toscolano-Maderno 68
Travedona 26
Tremezzo 42
Tremosine 69

Umbrella Museum 21

Val Camonica 54
Val Cannobina 19
Val Cavargna 34
Val Perlana 41
Val Rezzo 34
Val Veddasca 24
Valcuvia 25
Valsassina 48
Valsolda 32
Valtenesi 67
Varenna 47
Varese 26
Varesotto 26–7
Varone Waterfall 58
Verbania 19–20
Verona 74–7
Arche degli
Scaligeri 75
Arena 75
Basilica
Sant'Anastasia 76
Biblioteca Capitulare 76
Casa di Giulietta 75
Castelvecchio 75
Palazzo Giusti 76
Piazza dei Signori 75
Piazza delle Erbe 75
San Giorgio
Maggiore 76
San Zeno Maggiore ..77
Santa Maria
in Organo 76
Santa Maria
Matricolare 76
Teatro Romano 76
Tomba di Giulietta ...77
Villa Carlotta 42
Villa d'Este 40
Villa Giulia 44–5
Villa Melzi 45
Villa Monastero 47–8
Villa Pallavicino 21
Villa Pliniana 43
Villa Serbelloni 45
Villa Taranto 20
Voltorre 26

Wine 86

Zone 54